VICKERS
WELLINGTON

1936 to 1953 (all marks and models)

First published in 2012

A catalogue record for this book is available from the British Library.

ISBN 978 0 85733 230 1

Library of Congress control no. 2012940566

Haynes North America Inc., 861 Lawrence Drive, Newbury Park, California 91320, USA.

Published by Haynes Publishing,
Sparkford, Yeovil, Somerset BA22 7JJ, UK

Tel: 01963 440635
Int. tel: +44 1963 440635
Website: www.haynes.com

Printed in Malaysia.

Acknowledgements

The author would like to thank all those who contributed to the text and images, especially Julian Temple, Andrew Lewis, John Lattimore, and Denis Corley (Brooklands Museum) for access to 'R for Robert' and the museum's photo and document libraries; Patrick Hassell (Rolls-Royce Heritage Trust) for detailed discussion on engines; Dave Weatherley at the Royal Navy Heritage Trust for photos of their Fairey Swordfish's Pegasus; Peter Elliott (RAF Museum); Roger Audis (9 Squadron historian); Dicky James (9 Squadron Association); Chris Henderson (617 Squadron Association); Mary Stopes-Roe, and many Wellington ground and aircrew. Special thanks to Ken Wallis who flew Wellingtons operationally; to Robin Holmes who achieved the impossible in recovering 'R for Robert' from Loch Ness; and to Norman Parker who built and repaired Wellingtons throughout the war – all of whom contributed enormously to the details of the text.

VICKERS WELLINGTON

1936 to 1953 (all marks and models)

Owners' Workshop Manual

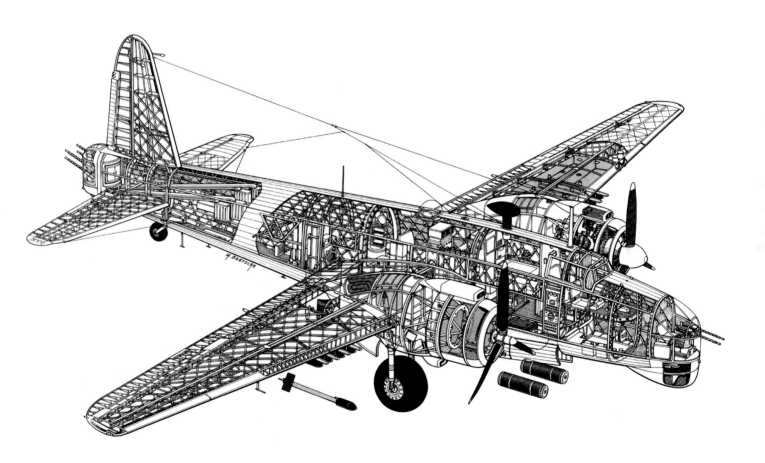

An insight into the history, development, production and role of the Second World War RAF bomber aircraft

Iain R. Murray

Contents

OPPOSITE N2980 'R for Robert' is lifted from Loch Ness in 1985 – this aircraft is now beautifully restored at Brooklands Museum. *(BAE Systems via Robin Holmes)*

Introduction

The Wellington was generally considered to be the best bomber in the RAF's armoury at the start of the Second World War and was so capable and adaptable that it was still in production at the end. It saw service with every RAF Command and in nearly every theatre of the war. This is the story of this remarkable aircraft.

OPPOSITE **The B.9/32 prototype, K4049, shows off at the 1936 RAF Display at Hendon; the family resemblance to the later Wellington is clear.** *(BAE Systems)*

The 'basketweave' bomber

As the storm clouds of war gathered during the 1930s, the nations of the world underwent a dramatic phase of rearmament, which resulted in new aircraft technologies being developed and produced for what many saw as the inevitable conflict to come.

The Vickers Wellington was created in this hectic time as the prime example of one of the new technologies – geodetic construction. A strange mix of modern structure with an old-school fabric covering, it looked complicated yet was so simple to mass-produce that it became the most numerous multi-engined aircraft ever built in Great Britain. Its unusual structure saw it dubbed the 'basketweave bomber' by the press, and the 'cloth bomber' by the sceptical Americans, yet this construction proved to be resilient in combat, with many severely damaged aircraft limping home to sing its praises.

The Wellington was to become the workhorse of Bomber and Coastal Commands, and also saw extensive service in the Middle East and in the Far East in a variety of roles. Although eclipsed by later four-engined aircraft, historian Max Hastings regards it as a 'brilliantly inspired piece of construction', which was 'undoubtedly one of the great aeroplanes of the war'.

The development of geodetics

In 1930, the Chief Designer of Vickers (Aviation) Ltd was the remarkable Reginald 'Rex' Pierson – having held the post since 1917, his prodigious output over this time had included the Vimy bomber, the Viastra airliner and the record-breaking Vespa. He was joined at the beginning of the year by Barnes Wallis, who was Britain's foremost airship designer, having designed the R80 and the recently completed R100 (although, following a successful maiden transatlantic voyage, the latter did not fly again, because of the crash of the competing R101). Even before the R100 flew, Wallis had taken up the post of Chief Designer (Structures) at Vickers to bring his expertise in light alloy construction to bear on heavier-than-air machines, and the two men would work together for the next 15 years, Pierson designing the form of the aircraft, and Wallis implementing the structure.

One innovative feature of R100 had been the wiring for holding its gasbags in position; the gasbags were mostly tapering cylinders to hold the largest possible volume of gas. To retain the bags in this shape, Wallis produced a novel wiring harness, strung between pairs of transverse ring frames, each wire tracing the shortest path around the curved outer surface of the gasbag – a geodesic line.

After starting work on aircraft structures, with projects such as a new wing for the Viastra, the tail of the prototype Jockey fighter, and a complete aircraft to Air Ministry specification M.1/30, Wallis realised that he could combine his two areas of expertise – using a network of light alloy struts formed in the curved shape of the outer surface to produce a new structural form, which he called geodetics (and which the company initially called Vickers-Wallis construction). The arrangement of the geodetic members to form the external aerodynamic shape would give the structure great strength for its weight, as the geodetics follow the shortest distance between two points in the curved surface, and with few internal structural components required, it would also offer large unobstructed internal volumes – ideal for payload or fuel tanks.

The theory of geodetics

Geodetics is based on the theory that if two curved members intersect at right angles, and one is subject to an inward force, then the other will translate this to an equal outward force – the so-called 'prop effect'. If this force is transmitted to another member parallel to the first, and so on, then a complete structure is formed in which the members in one direction brace and support the members running in the other direction, giving it great strength and rigidity even without internal bracing. The members themselves are also subject to bending forces, but as long as they have a small amount of depth and stiffness, then these forces are also carried with little difficulty, and this allows the material to carry a greater proportion of its theoretical strength than other construction methods would allow before buckling.

Geodetics were shown to be more efficient than a conventional articulated structure, and also gave 'all the spatial and formative advantages of a stressed skin and a large share of its inherent rigidity combined with the high developable stress of the articulated type'. Geodetic construction was estimated to give at least a 3% saving in weight over other forms, while offering a usable internal volume some 33% larger than articulated structures, a structural excellence that Wallis described as 'a beautiful thing'.

Geodetics were found to be particularly resistant to torsional (twisting) forces, though less resistant to bending forces, and even less to shear forces. For this reason, a pure geodetic structure was impractical, and it was found necessary to include longerons within the structure, and to have terminal frames at the ends (increasing structure weight slightly). On the Wellington, additional intermediate bulkhead frames were included to better spread the shear forces (resulting from point loads, such as wing attachments) across the geodetic framework. In wing structures, the flattened shape made the shear problem more acute, and spanwise wing spars had to be included to carry the lift shear forces.

Because of the inherent flexibility of the geodetic structure, the covering could not be rigid, so linen fabric was used – this being doped to keep it taught and make it waterproof, before being painted.

Manufacturing the geodetics

Despite the advantages of geodetic construction, there still remained the problem of mass production. At first glance, geodetics appears to be a complex system – many at the Air Ministry expressed opposition to it for this reason – and the draughtsmen who were tasked with preparing drawings must have had their skills tested. However, on closer inspection, the system is actually quite straightforward, with large sections of the airframe built from plain tubes and members of standard channel section, connected by a small

number of standard fixture types. Nevertheless, mass production did pose some challenges, though these were overcome by the sterling efforts of Trevor Westbrook (brought in at the end of 1936 from the Vickers subsidiary of Supermarine, where he had been General Manager and had initiated mass production of the Spitfire) and his staff.

Key to the rapid production of the geodetic members was the development of a forming machine that could take flat metal strip, roll it up into the required Σ-section and bend it to the required curvature, all in one continuous operation. The forming was done by a row of

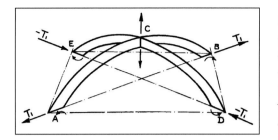

LEFT The basic geodetic node – an outward force in one curved member is balanced by an inward force in the other. *(BAE Systems via RAF Museum B3251)*

BELOW The patent drawing of the geodetic rolling machine. Strip enters at the top and is progressively formed into the final section in one operation, curvature being controlled by the settings of the cam wheels on the left. *(BAE Systems)*

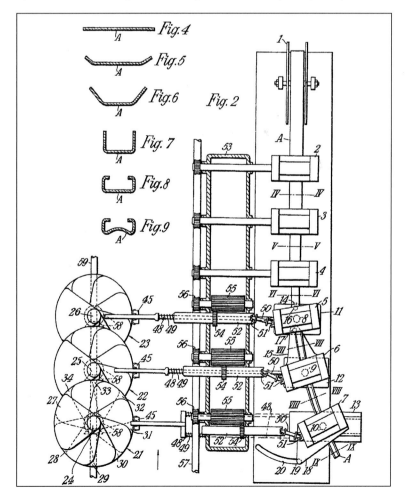

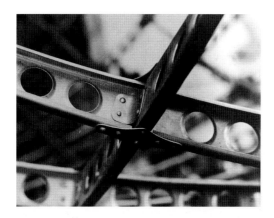

between five and seven pairs of rollers through which the strip passed, each pair adding an additional bend to the material. The last three rollers could be adjusted out of line via a series of cams, which could be preset with the required curvature (dependent on where the member was to go on the aircraft, and could even be varied along the length of a member) – a mechanical precursor to today's computer-controlled machine tools. The forming machines were developed primarily by Jack East and Charles Smith and patented in 1938 (GB503413) – by the following year, they were rolling over 1½ miles of strip per week at Weybridge, and they were so useful and adaptable that they were still being used for the

manufacture of BAC 1-11 and Concorde frame components into the 1970s.

The spatial definition of the nodal points in the structure was calculated by Basil Stephenson in the Drawing Office – all members were made to the same cross-section, but thickness varied from 12 to 22 SWG depending on the strength required. After being rolled, heat-treated and cut to length, the members were clamped to a steel 'boilerplate' jig to be drilled as required, and notches half the width of the member were cut out at each point of intersection. Small butterfly fittings were riveted into the notches, and the members were passed for assembly into panel sections, usually by subcontractors outwith the main factory, bolts being passed through each pair of butterfly fittings and a gusset plate riveted over the open end of the notch on each side. The completed sections were then sent back to the main factory to be joined together in a jig, an entire fuselage being assembled in less than 24 hours; all of this could be done by semi-skilled labour. The Wellington used some 1,650 separate geodetic members with 2,800 butterfly fittings and 650 longeron gussets all held together by 35,000 rivets.

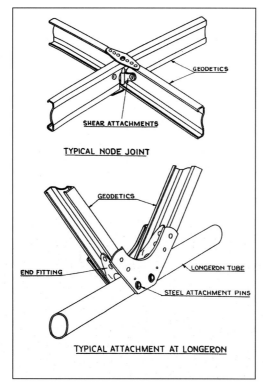

GEODETICS

SHEAR ATTACHMENTS

TYPICAL NODE JOINT

GEODETICS

END FITTING

LONGERON TUBE

STEEL ATTACHMENT PINS

TYPICAL ATTACHMENT AT LONGERON

The Wellesley

Wallis was given an opportunity to try out his ideas with the release of Air Ministry specification G.4/31 for a multi-purpose day- and torpedo-bomber, able to carry the (then substantial) bomb load of 2,000lb; it was to be a single-engined biplane. In addition to the biplane design, which incorporated a geodetic fuselage, Wallis proposed that a monoplane was also developed, using a similar fuselage but with the addition of a geodetic wing, and Vickers agreed to fund the development of this as a private venture (as it was without Air Ministry support).

To give good cruising efficiency, wings need to be long – but longer wings are subject to greater forces (notably torsion) than shorter wings, and this was the limiting factor of conventional wings. As a geodetic tube is resistant to torsional (twisting) deflection, this allowed Wallis to design a wing with a high aspect ratio (i.e. long span for a given chord length) of nearly 9:1. The long span reduced induced drag and thus extended range. However, as a wing is a flattened tube, the geodetic structure alone was not sufficiently strong in shear strength, and a conventional spanwise main spar was included (this was forked into a Y-shape inboard to form an undercarriage bay). The fuselage was formed from two opposing helices, braced by four longerons running fore-and-aft.

A comparison was made between the G.4/31 and the company's previous service design, the Vincent, which had a conventional articulated frame. Both aircraft had a similar all-up weight, but the Wellesley's structure weighed only two-thirds that of the Vincent. The fuselage and wings were tested for strength by adding weights to simulate flying loads; aircraft were required to survive a load factor of five times the maximum expected flight loading. The Vincent only just managed this load factor, but the G.4/31's fuselage reached a factor of 8, and the wings had reached over 11 before the test was stopped as the test rig was in danger of breaking first! The G.4/31 exhibited approximately half the torsional deflection of the Vincent, despite its lighter structure.

The biplane, K2771, was powered by a 625hp Bristol Pegasus and was ready by the late summer of 1934, being flown from Brooklands by Vickers' Chief Test Pilot, Joseph 'Mutt' Summers, before going for trials at both the A&AEE at Martlesham and the RAE at Farnborough.

BELOW The part-geodetic G.4/31 biplane flew in the summer of 1934, but was outperformed by its monoplane sibling. *(Author's collection)*

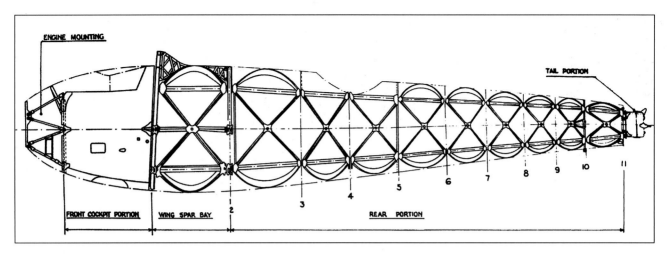

ENGINE MOUNTING

TAIL PORTION

FRONT COCKPIT PORTION   WING SPAR BAY   2   3   4   5   6   7   8   9   10   11   REAR PORTION

The G.4/31 monoplane, K7556, flew in June 1935, some ten months after the biplane and using the same type of engine, but tests showed that the monoplane was lighter and able to demonstrate a substantially better performance, even when more heavily loaded than the biplane. Despite this, the Air Ministry pressed on with an order for 150 biplanes, but the Vickers Chairman, Sir Robert Maclean, unilaterally switched this to monoplanes, and the Air Ministry reluctantly made it official on 10 September; it was to be called the Wellesley (in honour of Arthur Wellesley, the Duke of Wellington, and indirectly in honour of Wallis, as all other Vickers aircraft had official names beginning with 'V').

Following a minor accident during testing, K7556 was rebuilt as the pre-production prototype Wellesley, to a revised specification as a day bomber (the general-purpose and torpedo-bombing roles having been dropped). This included cockpit hoods, hydraulically operated undercarriage and a faired tail wheel. To avoid the large cut-out in the geodetics which a bomb bay would have required, Wallis designed two panniers to fit under the wings, each capable of carrying two 500lb bombs. Initially, these were fitted with bomb doors, but these caused excessive vibrations when opened, so the doors were deleted with little effect on aerodynamic performance.

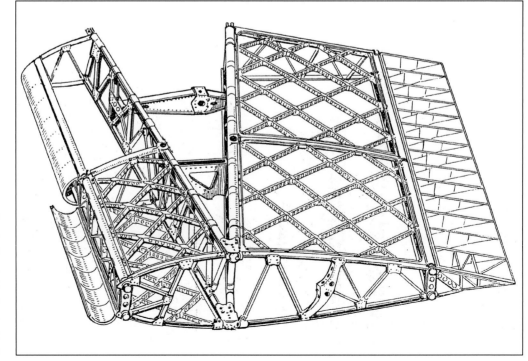

The Wellesley in service

The first production Wellesley flew on 30 January 1937, and the third aircraft was delivered to 76 Squadron at RAF Finningley on 22 March. It equipped five Bomber Command squadrons by the start of 1938 and the last of the 176 Wellesleys was delivered in May. However, even before the outbreak of war, it was recognised that the aircraft was obsolescent, and within 18 months, all service aircraft were transferred to the Middle East. Here they saw action against Italian forces in Sudan, Eritrea and Abyssinia (now Ethiopia), undertaking bombing, strafing, general reconnaissance, and policing duties. Only two squadrons were still using the aircraft by the start of 1942, and the last was withdrawn from service in March 1943. Only one production mark was built, although there were some conversions to an unofficial Mk II and some were used as test beds.

Long-range flight

The Wellesley's 'finest hour' probably came in 1938 at the hands of the RAF's Long Range Development Unit, which had been formed with a view to regaining the World Distance Record. The unit had achieved success with the Fairey Long Range Monoplane in 1933, flying from the UK to Namibia, but France and then Russia had subsequently captured the record, and it was recognised that the Wellesley could be capable of taking the record back again.

Four standard Wellesleys were fitted with more powerful Pegasus XXII engines (these had a higher compression ratio and a smaller supercharger optimised for flight at 10,000ft)

with aerodynamic cowlings, extra internal tankage (bringing the total fuel load up to 1,290 gallons, making up more than half the total weight of the aircraft), and other special modifications. Trial flights from England to Egypt and back were made in July 1938, then on 5 November three aircraft under the command of Sqn Ldr Richard Kellett departed from Ismailia in Egypt and 48 hours later arrived in Darwin, Australia (though one was forced to land at Koepang in West Timor to refuel) – a new record distance of 7,158.6 miles, which would stand until broken by a Boeing B-29 Superfortress more than seven years later.

The Wellington prototype – B.9/32

The Wellington story begins with the publication in September 1932 of Air Ministry specification B.9/32 for a two-engined all-metal day bomber able to carry a bomb load of 1,000lb for 720 miles. Initially the tare weight was limited to 6,300lb to comply with League of Nations agreements, but this restriction was eventually lifted, and after various layouts and engines had been considered, a design was submitted in February 1933 with 560hp Rolls-Royce Goshawk engines and an all-up weight of 11,400lb. A revised specification was issued in June 1934, and following further specification alterations, the aircraft was completed as an all-geodetic mid-wing bomber with a wing aspect ratio of nearly 9:1, two 915hp Bristol Pegasus X engines and an all-up weight of 21,000lb. Modern features included single gun mountings in the nose, tail, dorsal, and

ABOVE A Wellesley of 47 Squadron on active service over Eritrea in April 1941. *(Author's collection)*

ventral positions (though guns were not actually fitted), retractable undercarriage, variable-pitch airscrews, and a large bomb bay; top speed was 250mph at 8,000ft.

The new aircraft, K4049, was christened Crécy on 5 June 1936 and made its maiden flight from Brooklands ten days later in the hands of 'Mutt' Summers, with Wallis and Westbrook along as passengers. An initial production order for 180 aircraft followed two weeks later, and brought with it a new name – Wellington (the reasons for the name change are unclear). The prototype underwent trials from Weybridge before being sent to the A&AEE in November for further tests, achieving a maximum altitude of 19,200ft. Handling was found to be similar at all weights, and the aircraft was generally found to be satisfactory,

with single-engine performance and cockpit comfort being 'commendable'. A tendency to fly nose-up with flaps down was noted, and the main wheel brakes needed immediate improvement. Near the end of the planned test programme in April 1937, the aircraft crashed during diving trials, killing the observer G.P. Smurthwaite, although the pilot, Maurice Hare, parachuted to safety. The cause was traced to elevator overbalance.

The B.9/32 prototype design had never been intended for mass production, but was essentially to show that an aircraft the size of the Wellington could be constructed using the geodetic principle and, despite the crash, had shown that this was both possible and as structurally efficient as had been hoped. The B.9/32 demonstrated that it was capable of

BELOW The B.9/32 prototype demonstrated that a large geodetic bomber was not only practical, but also a potential world-beater. Here it is being run up on the Brooklands racetrack outside the factory. *(BAE Systems)*

carrying a load of 4,500lb over a range of 2,800 miles – each figure four times what the original specification had called for. The production redesign of the structure to specification B.29/36 followed the same general form as the prototype, but internally, details of the structure were different: the geodetic channels were not perforated, the longerons were moved from their positions at the top, bottom, and sides to the side panels (to improve the carrying of bending forces and for ease of manufacture), the dorsal gun position fittings were deleted and the tail fin and rudder were redesigned (the prototype had used one of the twin fins from a Supermarine Stranraer to save time). There were some minor additional differences – the nose was extended slightly, the rear fuselage was deepened by removing the tapering section which also raised the fin by 6in, the horizontal stabiliser was redesigned, the main wheel doors were changed, and the tail wheel was made retractable. Provision was made for cabin heating and de-icing (though these were not actually fitted until the Mk II). Consideration was also given to fitting dual controls. Engines were to be supercharged Pegasus XVIIIs (or XXs if the XVIIIs were not ready) driving constant-speed propellers.

Production

Well before the war started, the government had realised the benefits (both in dispersal and increased capacity) of having war materiel built in different places, and implemented the 'shadow factory' scheme. Development and initial production would take place at a parent factory, but once a design was frozen and production was established, this would be duplicated in one or more subsidiary locations. Most shadow factories were built by the government and managed by motor manufacturers, but Vickers managed their own new factory beside Hawarden airfield and the village of Broughton, near Chester (it being known by all three names), and it produced its first Wellington, N2761, in August 1939. This was followed by a second factory at Squires Gate airfield, south of Blackpool, and its first aircraft, X3160, was completed in September 1940. All the factories used locally recruited

semi-skilled labour, much of the workforce at all the factories being women. Dispersal was further continued by having many small firms fabricate or assemble parts, which were then taken to the main factory for final assembly; this was accelerated at Weybridge after the factory was bombed by the Luftwaffe in September 1940, over 500 subcontractors ultimately being used. Broughton operated entirely as an assembly plant, with no on-site fabrication of parts. Geodetic panels were one example of parts that were assembled by subcontractors, some even having the geodetic rolling machines in-house (three produced all the geodetics for Broughton). Each factory also had a second production line located nearby – Smith's Lawn in Windsor Great Park (known as VAX1) about eight miles to the north-west of Weybridge, Cranage near Broughton, and Stanley Park near Blackpool. Weybridge had two other main sites – the Experimental Department was based at Foxwarren a mile to the south-east, and the airfield at Wisley three miles to the south. The shadow factory scheme was also applied to engine manufacture (see Chapter 4).

All apparatus – including bomb beams, radios, radar, and aerials – was normally fitted on the production line, the only exception being guns (and ammunition). Early aircraft were delivered direct to squadrons, but during the war, normal practice was to deliver them to Maintenance Units where armament was fitted, then they were ferried to their squadrons from there.

Prototypes and special variants were tested at Weybridge by a small team of test pilots under 'Mutt' Summers, and also at A&AEE and RAE. Rolls-Royce undertook a lot of engine testing from their own site at Hucknall. With several new aircraft being completed at each factory every day (at its peak, Broughton alone was building 28 aircraft a week), production test flying was intense, and RAF pilots resting after an operational tour were employed as test pilots utilising the runways at the main factories; much of Weybridge's moving to the longer runway at Wisley when that opened in 1944.

With production techniques decided upon, geodetic-rolling machines operational, and shadow factories tooling up, by the start of 1939 the stage was set for rapid production of the Wellington.

Chapter One

The Wellington Story

In production throughout the Second World War, fourteen primary variants of the Wellington were built and there were a further six main converted variants. Smaller numbers were also used in a wide variety of other roles and as a test-bed aircraft for many more. The larger Warwick and the post-war Viking airliner were also based on the Wellington.

OPPOSITE An early-type 4,000lb HC 'Cookie' is being loaded on to a Mk III – the Wellington was the first aircraft to drop this type of bomb. *(IWM TR11)*

Theme and variations – the Wellington marks

The main marks and their principal differences are given in the following list; there were typically many minor changes between and within marks as well. Variants were also assigned different Type numbers by Vickers. It was often the case that two or more marks were in production at the same time, even at the same factory, sometimes with alternate aircraft being different marks. Further details on numbers built at each factory can be found in Appendix 2.

Mk I – Types 285 (pre-production), 290 (production), 403 (New Zealand variant)

The first pre-production Mk I Wellington, L4212, was fitted with Pegasus XX engines and flew in December 1937, undergoing a flight test programme which mainly focused on general stability and engine and undercarriage performance, with two weeks at RAE in January 1938 for resonance tests, this ending prematurely when the starboard landing gear collapsed on landing in February. While undergoing repairs, the Pegasus XVIII engines (850hp) with two-speed supercharger arrived and these were installed. Other changes included fitting a new undercarriage pump, side windows, and a Frazer-Nash ventral turret. When flying was resumed at the end of April, the new engines gave a marked improvement, and on its 22nd flight, it was flown to Martlesham for official approval to allow production to commence. Stability and engine tests then continued at Weybridge until moving to Eastleigh in July, being joined by L4213 in August. These tests resulted in various modifications being implemented, including fitting of horn-balanced elevators in place of the tab-balanced originals, and the ASI pitot head was moved from the fuselage to the starboard wing. Gun turret trials (including the ventral FN turret) were carried out with L4212 in February 1939.

The Mk I was primarily distinguished by having Vickers front and rear turrets (see Chapter 3); a Frazer-Nash ventral turret had been specified by the Air Ministry, but it is believed that this was only fitted to the pre-production aircraft.

Mk IA – Types 408 (production), 412 (New Zealand variant)

Because of problems with the Vickers turrets, these were replaced by Frazer-Nash FN.5 turrets, each with two .303 Brownings; an FN.25 retractable ventral turret was also fitted. The airframe was stressed for an AUW of 28,000lb and (to provide the option of fitting different engine types later) 'power egg' nacelles were fitted (though the engines remained Pegasus XVIIIs meantime). Larger main wheels were fitted to handle the increased weight, the oxygen system was revised, and a flotation system was added.

Mk IB – Type 409

This was a proposed Mk IA with the addition of beam guns to make up for deficiencies in the turret armament, but it was superseded by the IC before any were built.

BELOW Family tree of Wellington main marks, derivatives and conversions. *(Author)*

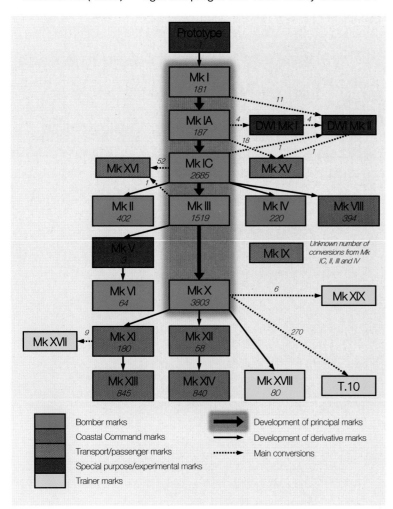

Bomber marks
Coastal Command marks
Transport/passenger marks
Special purpose/experimental marks
Trainer marks

→ Development of principal marks
→ Development of derivative marks
⋯⋯► Main conversions

BELOW Looking down towards the unused ventral turret fitting, which is filled by a frame and covered with walkway boarding. *(Author)*

Mk IC – Type 415

Based on early experience, numerous changes were made to the IA, leading to the IC. The ventral turret was deleted, as its effectiveness was questionable (although a few early examples may have retained this turret). For defence from beam attack, it was replaced by manually operated guns in the rear fuselage, either drum-fed Vickers K guns or belt-fed .303 Brownings. These were originally in the after part of the side window strip, but later they were given their own trapezoidal windows further aft. A more powerful hydraulic system, driven by a Vickers Variable Speed Gear (VSG) pump, was fitted to give 300psi for turret hydraulics and 1,000psi for other services, the 12V electrical system was replaced with a 24V system, and a DR compass was installed. The IC took part in its first operation on 20 March 1940; it was the first mature variant of the Wellington, with more than three-quarters of the Pegasus-engined Wellingtons being ICs.

Mk II – Types 298 (prototype), 406 (production)

The Mk II was virtually identical to the Mk IC apart from its engines, which were 1,145hp Merlin Xs. The centre-of-gravity change caused by the heavier engine required ballasting changes and

the main gear was moved forward 3in in the down position by extending the backstays. After flight tests, the chord of the horizontal tailplane was increased to improve fore-and-aft stability by extending the ribs forward by 12in inboard, tapering to nil at the tips. The airscrews rotated in the opposite direction to the Pegasus, and this was found to alter the airflow over the tail surfaces, slightly changing the handling. However, with more power available, the Mk II delivered a performance advantage over the IC. Cabin heating was fitted, and plastic ice guards (36in x 20in) were added under the fuselage fabric to give protection from ice thrown off the propellers. The first Type 423 conversions for the 4,000lb 'Cookie' were Mk IIs, and some were also used for weapons and other trials. The prototype Mk II flew in March 1939 but delivery of production machines did not start until 18 months later and, because of restricted Merlin availability, only 402 were produced (all at Weybridge).

Mk III – Types 299 (prototype), 417 (production)

The Mk III was also based on the IC, but used Bristol Hercules engines (initially 1,400hp IIIs, later 1,590hp XIs), and most used Rotol electric propellers. It was the first mark to be fitted with a four-gun FN.20A tail turret (a two-gun FN.4 was used on early aircraft because of delays with the FN.20A) and the beam guns were retained. Other additions included extra armour plating, balloon cable cutters on the leading edges, and windscreen wipers. AUW was increased from 28,000lb in early Mk IIIs to 34,500lb in later aircraft. Deliveries started in autumn 1940 and 1,519 were built before it was superseded by the Mk X as the main bomber variant.

Mk IV – Types 410 (prototype), 424 (production)

The Mk IV was based on the Mk III but with 1,050hp Pratt & Whitney Twin Wasp radial engines. Hamilton standard propellers were used on the prototype, but were found to be very noisy, so Curtiss electric propellers were substituted on the production aircraft. Because of limited engine availability, only 220 were built (all at Broughton).

Mk V – Types 407, 421, 426, 436

The Mk V with Hercules VIII engines was developed from 1938 as a high-altitude bomber, to deliver a 1,000lb bomb load from 40,000ft. A pressure cabin was added for the crew of three, inset into the top of the front

fuselage. Numerous troubles were encountered in testing, many caused by the cold conditions at altitude, but the main problem was the lack of power from the engines, which prevented the aircraft from reaching the desired altitude. Only three were built, two at Foxwarren and one at VAX1, other airframes under construction being completed as Mk VIAs.

Mk VI – Types 431 (prototype), 442 (production VIA), 449 (production VIG)

The Mk VI was the Merlin-engined successor to the Mk V, but the Merlin 60 also gave some problems. These were eventually overcome along with other difficulties of high-altitude flight, and a total of 64 aircraft were built.

For more information on the Mk V and Mk VI, see 'High-altitude Wellingtons'.

Mk VII – Type 430

This would have been a Mk II fitted with more powerful Merlin XX engines, but other aircraft were given priority for these engines and the prototype was cancelled before completion (becoming a Merlin 60 test bed).

Mk VIII – Type 429 (production)

The Mk VIII was a variant of the Mk IC modified for General Reconnaissance with Coastal Command. They were clearly distinguished by the dipole aerials on the rear fuselage and the Yagi aerials beneath the outer wings belonging to the Air-to-Surface Vessel (ASV) Mk II radar for detecting ships and surfaced U-boats. Of nearly 400 built, most were equipped as torpedo bombers for daylight operations, and 58 were equipped with the Leigh Light for night operations. All retained a two-gun rear turret, and torpedo aircraft also kept their nose turret while others had an unarmed observation nose based on the cupola of the Mk I. These aircraft were all built at Weybridge, being interspersed with Mk ICs on the production line.

Mk IX – Type 437 (all conversions)

This was the formal designation applied to an unknown number of Mk IC, II, III and IV aircraft converted to carry 18 troops or equivalent payload, with turrets replaced by fairings (which had originally been designed to allow Wellingtons to be flight-tested when turrets were not available).

Mk X – Type 440 (production)

The Mk X was the ultimate bomber variant of the Wellington, being a further development of the Mk III, from which it was virtually indistinguishable. It was the most numerous variant built (ultimately making up one-third of all Wellingtons), all coming from the two shadow factories (Weybridge continued to produce Coastal Command marks and the Warwick); RP590, the final Wellington delivered in October 1945, was a Mk X.

Structural strength was improved from the Mk III by utilising a new aluminium alloy DTD646. This ingeniously allowed the fuselage structure to be strengthened while being manufactured in exactly the same way, increasing the all-up weight without increasing structure weight. Hercules VI or XVI engines of 1,675hp were fitted, these having carburettors with automatic mixture control giving the Mk X the best performance of any Wellington. Initially, tail turrets were FN.20A, and subsequently FN.120 or FN.121.

Mk XI – Types 454/459 (prototypes), 458 (production)

The Mk XI was a Coastal Command 'day' variant superseding the Mk VIII but based on the Mk X airframe, with Hercules VI or XVI engines; beam guns, torpedo equipment, and ASV Mk II were fitted on most aircraft.

Mk XII – Type 455

The Mk XII was a 'night' variant of the Mk XI additionally fitted with a Leigh Light and Mk I-style nose cupola and carrying depth charges only. In later aircraft, ASV Mk II was replaced by ASV Mk III in a nose radome.

Mk XIII – Type 466

The Mk XIII was a Mk XI with 1,735hp Hercules XVII engines better suited to low-level operation. In later aircraft, ASV Mk II was replaced by ASV Mk III.

Mk XIV – Type 467

The Mk XIV was a Mk XII with Hercules XVII engines. All had ASV Mk III and Leigh Light.

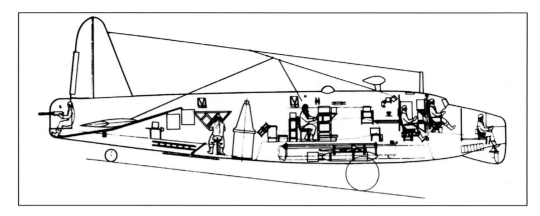

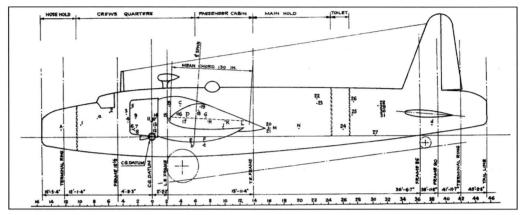

Mk XV/Mk XVI – no Type designations (all conversions)

These two marks were troop transport conversions – XV from Mk IAs (18 aircraft) and

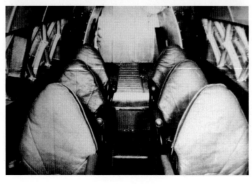

XVI from Mk ICs (52 aircraft) plus at least one converted from a Mk III. Between the main spar and trailing edge frame was a cabin for up to six passengers, aft of which was a main hold for up to 1,300lb of cargo (only 400lb with six passengers) and aft of that a toilet. A personnel door was created on the starboard side aft of the (deleted) flare chute. Both turrets were replaced by fairings; the nose fairing was used as a hold for up to 350lb of additional cargo.

Mk XVII – Type 487 (all conversions)

This designation was applied to nine service conversions of Mk XI aircraft as Airborne Interception (AI) radar trainers. The aircraft was fitted with an SCR720 AI radome, as fitted to Mosquito nightfighters, in place of the front turret.

Mk XVIII – Type 490

Mk XVIIIs had the same equipment as the Mk XVII with accommodation for up to four trainees plus an instructor. Eighty of this variant were built (all at Blackpool).

Mk XIX – no Type designation (all conversions)

The Mk XIX was a post-war service conversion of Mk Xs to act as basic trainers. The front turret was replaced by a fairing, and although the rear turret was retained, it was inactive with guns and hydraulics removed. Colour was silver overall with yellow bands around fuselage and wings to denote their training status. Twenty-four aircraft were earmarked for conversion at 24 MU at Stoke Heath in Shropshire, but only six were converted. After testing, all went into storage at Aston Down, and were then scrapped without being used.

T.10 – Type 619 (all conversions)

The T.10s were also post-war conversions of Mk Xs as navigation training aircraft similar to the Mk XIX, but the 270 conversions were performed by Boulton-Paul at Wolverhampton between 1946 and 1952, the aircraft being stripped, overhauled, and recovered. T.10s had dual controls, and had a navigator's station (including a second Gee installation) aft of the main spar for two navigators and an instructor, Lockheed hydraulic pumps and horn-balanced rudders, with extra aerials for the additional navigation aids. T.10s were the last Wellingtons to fly with the RAF, some remaining in service until 1953 when they were replaced in the training role by Valettas and Varsitys.

ABOVE MF628 is a late B.X, later converted to a T.10 trainer and now preserved in the RAF Museum. *(Chris England/Air-Britain Historians)*

MAIN PARTICULARS – EARLY WELLINGTON MARKS

	Prototype B.9/32	Mk I	Mk IC	Mk II
Span	85ft 10in	86ft	86ft 2in	86ft 2in
Length	60ft 6in	61ft 3in	64ft 7in	64ft 7in
Height*	14ft 3in	17ft 5in	17ft 5in	17ft 5in
Empty weight	12,260lb	18,000lb	18,550lb	20,250lb
Gross weight	21,000lb	24,850lb	28,500lb	33,000lb
Max. speed	250mph at 8,000ft	245mph at 15,000ft	235mph at 15,500ft	254mph at 17,500ft
Max. bomb load	4,500lb est.	4,500lb	4,500lb	4,000lb
Service ceiling	19,200ft	21,600ft	18,000ft	23,500ft
Range	2,800 miles	3,200 miles at 180mph/15,000ft	2,550 miles at 180mph/15,000ft	2,200 miles at 180mph/15,000ft
Engines x 2	Pegasus X, 915hp	Pegasus XVIII, 1,050hp	Pegasus XVIII, 1,050hp	Merlin X, 1,145hp

* To top of tail with all wheels on ground.

For details of turrets and bomb loads, see Chapter 3. Particulars of other marks are similar to those they were derived from.

	Proto	I	IA	IC	II	III	IV	V	VI	VIII	IX	X	XI	XII	XIII	XIV	XV	XVI	XVII	XVIII	XIX	T.10	DWI
COLOUR SCHEME																							
Silver overall	✔																				✔	✔	
Yellow trainer bands																					✔	✔	
Fuselage upper and sides, wings upper: dark earth/dark brown camouflage Fuselage and wings underside: black		✔								✔							✔	✔					✔
Fuselage and wings upper: dark earth/dark brown camouflage Fuselage sides and underside, wings underside: black			✔	✔	✔	✔	✔	✔	✔	✔	✔	✔			✔				✔	✔			✔
Fuselage and wings upper: dark earth/dark brown camouflage Fuselage sides and underside, wings underside: white									✔			✔	✔	✔	✔								
Fuselage and wings upper: slate grey Fuselage sides and underside, wings underside: white												✔	✔	✔	✔								
ENGINES																							
Bristol Pegasus (exhausts outboard)	✔	✔	✔	✔						✔	✔												✔
Rolls-Royce Merlin (stub exhausts)					✔				✔														
Bristol Hercules (exhausts inboard)						✔		✔				✔	✔	✔	✔	✔	✔	✔	✔	✔	✔		
Pratt & Whitney Twin Wasp (exhausts both sides)							✔																
TURRETS																							
Vickers turrets nose (1 gun) and tail (2 guns)		✔																					
FN.5 nose (2 guns)		✔	✔	✔	✔	✔				✔		✔											
FN.5 tail (2 guns)		✔	✔	✔						✔													
FN.20A/120/121 tail (4 guns)						✔	✔	✔	✔			✔	✔	✔	✔	✔			✔	✔			
Vickers turret-type nose glazing (0 or 1 gun)										✔			✔	✔	✔	✔							
FN.25 ventral turret (2 guns)		✔																					
FN.77 ventral turret with Leigh Light										✔			✔		✔								
Turrets replaced by fairings	✔										✔							✔	✔		✔	✔	✔
EXTERNAL FEATURES																							
Astrodome			✔	✔	✔	✔	✔			✔	✔	✔	✔	✔	✔	✔	✔	✔	✔	✔	✔	✔	
Two aerial masts, unfaired DF loop		✔																					
One aerial mast, faired DF loop			✔	✔	✔	✔	✔	✔	✔	✔	✔	✔	✔	✔	✔	✔	✔	✔	✔	✔	✔	✔	✔
Waist guns			✔							✔		✔	✔	✔	✔								
Pressure cabin in nose, long fairing beneath								✔	✔														
Pressure cabin in nose, short fairing beneath									✔														
ASV Mk II aerial masts										✔		✔	✔	✔									
ASV Mk II radome under-nose turret													✔	✔	✔								
AI radar dome in nose fairing																			✔	✔			
DWI coil																							✔
INTERNAL FEATURES																							
12V electrical system	✔	✔	✔																				✔
24V electrical system				✔	✔	✔	✔	✔	✔	✔	✔	✔	✔	✔	✔	✔	✔	✔	✔	✔	✔	✔	
VSG hydraulics, DR compass			✔	✔	✔	✔	✔	✔	✔	✔	✔	✔	✔	✔	✔	✔	✔	✔	✔	✔	✔	✔	
Strengthened alloy												✔	✔	✔	✔	✔	✔	✔	✔	✔	✔	✔	
Passenger seating											✔						✔	✔					
Trainee seating																			✔	✔	✔	✔	
Torpedo equipment										✔		✔		✔									

This chart shows the most commonly seen features of the various marks of Wellington.

MAIN PARTICULARS –
LATER WELLINGTON MARKS AND WARWICK

	Mk III	Mk VI	Mk X	Warwick ASR Mk I
Span	86ft 2in	86ft 2in	86ft 2in	96ft 8in
Length	64ft 7in	61ft 9in	64ft 7in	72ft 3in
Height	17ft 6in	17ft 6in	17ft 6in	18ft 6in
Empty weight	21,050lb	20,280lb	22,475lb	28,150lb
Gross weight	up to 34,500lb	30,450lb	36,500lb	45,000lb
Max. speed	261mph at 12,500ft	300mph	255mph at 13,300ft	224mph at 3,600ft
Max. bomb load	4,000lb	4,500lb	4,000lb	—
Service ceiling	22,700ft	38,500ft	22,000ft	19,000ft
Range	2,040 miles at 180mph/15,000ft	2,275 miles	1,885 miles at 180mph/15,000ft	2,300 miles at 150mph/5,000ft
Engines x 2	Hercules III/XI, 1,425hp	Merlin 60, 1,600hp	Hercules VI/XVI, 1,675hp	Double Wasp, 1,850hp

For details of turrets and bomb loads, see Chapter 3. Particulars of other marks are similar to those they were derived from.

Wellington's twin – the Warwick

The Warwick is generally assumed to be the successor to the Wellington, but it is more correct to say that the Warwick is the Wellington's larger twin. When Wallis and Pierson were working on designs to meet specification B.1/35 for a heavy bomber, they realised that they could combine this with their production Wellington design to produce two aircraft with large sections common to both. The result was that the Wellington fuselage structure was essentially a Warwick fuselage with a 6ft section removed from the centre (this is reflected in the frame station numbering, which in the Warwick was continuous, but in the Wellington frames 27–37 were omitted with 26 and 38 overlapping); the wings of both aircraft outboard of the engine nacelles were identical. The largest structural difference was the Warwick's inner wing, which used a triple-tube spar for strength and the wing structure was unbroken by the nacelle, this being entirely below the wing. Span was increased by 10ft, tail surfaces were slightly enlarged and ventral and/or dorsal turrets were usually fitted. This common heritage is also evidenced by Vickers' numbering – the Warwick was Type 284 and the first production Wellington was Type 285.

It was expected that the smaller Wellington would be produced first, but that the Warwick would become the main production aircraft. However, the heavier Warwick required more powerful engines, and although Vickers preferred the Hercules, the Air Ministry specified the Rolls-Royce Vulture. Development delays with this engine (which also plagued the Avro Manchester) meant that the first Warwick did not fly until August 1939 – an incredible three years after the flight of the Wellington prototype. The ability to use the Napier Sabre and (later) Bristol Centaurus (a development of the Hercules) had also been requested by the Air Ministry (and common attachment points had been agreed between the three engine makers and Vickers), but the Sabre also experienced development delays. The first Centaurus Warwick flew in April 1940, and demonstrated better performance than its Vulture-engined stablemate, although some stability problems were also encountered. The Pratt & Whitney Double Wasp R-2800 engine was also added as an alternative, and production orders were

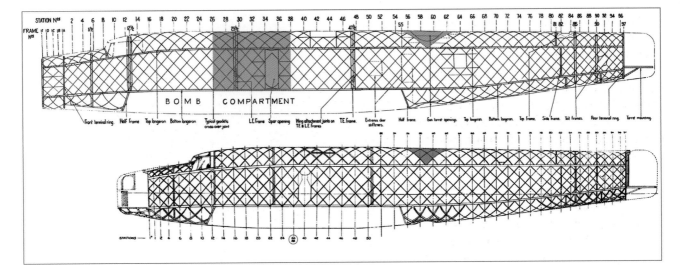

placed in January 1941 for 150 of these (designated Mk I) plus an additional 100 aircraft with the Centaurus (as the Mk II) – with the orders finally came the name for the aircraft, which had been the B.1/35 for six years! The stability problem was finally resolved in spring 1944 by adding a dorsal extension ahead of the fin, and this was retro-fitted to all earlier aircraft.

Although designed to carry a 50% larger bomb load than the Wellington, by the time the Warwick appeared it had already been superseded by the advent of the four-engined heavy bombers, and none ever served as a bomber. However, with its capacity and long

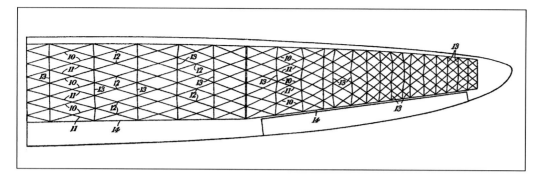

range, it saw extensive service in a number of other roles. Maritime reconnaissance aircraft were fitted with ASV Mk II or Mk III (the radome was mounted further aft than on the Wellington) and a Leigh Light. Its most common role was air-sea rescue (which the Wellington was tested for) in various versions, initially carrying Lindholme gear and later also carrying a motorised lifeboat protruding from the bomb bay. This equipment could be dropped by parachute near ditched aircrew. Fourteen Warwicks were produced as passenger transports for BOAC, and a hundred more as freighters, with a cargo pannier mated to the bomb bay and no turrets. In all, 846 Warwicks were built, taking over from Wellington production at Weybridge (which ceased in 1943) and continuing until the spring of 1946. As with the Wellington, many aircraft were used as development test beds for engines, weapons, and other features, but all remaining examples of the type were withdrawn in 1947.

Wellington developments – the Windsor

The ultimate development of the geodetic principle was the Windsor. Although externally a four-engined development of the two-engined Wellington/Warwick (in the same way that the Lancaster was a development of the Manchester), the Windsor was quite different underneath. Its wings were thick enough to be made without spars, and they were constructed as a single geodetic tube passing through, and interlinked with, the fuselage tube. The wings were a considerable production challenge as, unlike the earlier aircraft, the geodetic members were not all the same, being heavier at the wing root and becoming gradually thinner towards the tip; the

angles also varied, with the members being laid at 16° to spanwise at the root (where bending loads are greatest), but curving to 45° near the tip (where torsional loads are greatest) meaning that nearly every joint was unique. The Windsor used Wellington main wheels, one being fitted under each nacelle, giving the aircraft a unique appearance when on the ground; another novel feature was the use of defensive cannon mounted in barbettes on the rear of the outer engine nacelles and controlled remotely by a gunner in the tail of the aircraft.

As an alternative to fabric covering, which was prone to damage at high speed, Wallis developed an alternative flexible covering, made as a woven sheet of thin metal strips, this being oversprayed with a covering of PVC for weatherproofing, and this was fitted to one of the prototypes.

Three Windsors were built by the Experimental Department and first flown in October 1943, and although production orders were placed for the aircraft, these were cancelled when the war ended, and no more were built.

Wellington developments – the Viking

Geodetics did, however, have one final outing – although the Brabazon Committee of 1942 had looked ahead to post-war civil aircraft, it had given little consideration to aircraft to be used until the new generation was ready. Consequently, Vickers proposed an interim airliner that would utilise the wings from the Wellington and Warwick tail surfaces, mated to a new stressed-skin pressure-cabin fuselage; engines would be an improved variant of the Hercules. This heritage allowed rapid development and the VC.1 Viking first flew in June 1945 (the Vickers lineage returning to names beginning with 'V').

The first 19 aircraft used the standard Wellington wings, with later aircraft using new stressed-skin outer wings, although the inner wings retained the geodetic construction; as this section was reasonably rigid, it could be skinned with metal so the geodetics were not apparent. As with the Wellington transport variants, a passenger door was provided in the rear fuselage, which meant that passengers did not need to scramble over the main spar, which served as a divider between the passenger and crew sections. Although production ceased in 1948 after 163 Vikings had been built, the aircraft continued in service into the early 1960s, by which time the Viscount and its contemporaries had become established.

High-altitude Wellingtons

In 1938, the Air Ministry expressed an interest in developing aircraft to operate at high altitudes, with commercial applications to avoid bad weather at lower altitudes, and also bombers that would be immune from flak and fighter attacks at high altitude. The basic requirement was for an aircraft with an AUW of 28,000lb capable of carrying a 1,000lb load with fuel for nine hours' flying up to a ceiling of 40,000ft. To reach this height, the crew would need to be housed in a pressure-cabin, but the technology for this was in its infancy. The French were pioneers in pressure cabin research, and Pierson had already been in communication with Henri Farman. When the fall of France appeared imminent, company physicist Herbert Jeffree was dispatched to France to collect as much information on the research as he could. Several manufacturers tendered for the work, and in March 1939 Vickers were instructed to convert two Mk I Wellingtons. Because of the groundbreaking nature of the work, the DTD, RAE, Vickers, Shorts, Fairey, Bristol, and Rolls-Royce all agreed to share their research.

Pierson proposed a small pressure vessel set into the nose of a modified Wellington attached to the airframe at four points, and this was designed by Wallis (and patented – GB562301, GB565860, GB571719, and GB572303). This cabin (which was 18ft 3in long and 5ft 5in diameter) housed the pilot, navigator/bomb aimer, and wireless operator and maintained an atmospheric pressure equivalent to 10,000ft – hence if the aircraft flew at 40,000ft, the cabin would have to withstand a pressure differential of 7.5psi; it was tested to double that figure. An engine-driven blower maintained the pressure, and an emergency valve would open if the aircraft had to dive rapidly. The pilot's head protruded from the fuselage under a transparent dome, and a flat window for the bomb aimer was fitted in the nose (an American Sperry high-altitude bombsight was to be used), with smaller additional windows for the navigator to use for star fixes. Key to the success of the cabin was the selection of sealants to use both for the structure and the openings, and various products were tested – the ability to function down to −65°C was essential. The cabin was built from riveted sheet, with sealant sprayed on to the inside where internal pressure would force it into any gaps, and was heavily lagged to keep heat loss to a minimum.

Hercules- and Merlin-powered variants were developed as the Mk V and Mk VI respectively, priority initially being given to the Mk V. The Hercules VIII with a two-stage supercharger was to be used, but delays with this engine led to a Hercules III being fitted initially and prototype R3298 made its first flight with this engine in September 1940, with the first attempt at high altitude the following month. Most test flying was done from Blackpool as a dispersal precaution following the bombing at Weybridge, sometimes with as many as six on board. Three-bladed propellers were used with the Hercules III but all later high-altitude aircraft had four-bladed propellers to give more purchase on the thin air.

The second prototype R3299 made its first flight in May 1941 with Hercules VIII engines, but the new supercharger did not perform as expected, and it was not until January 1943 that 33,000ft was reached. Turbochargers were suggested to boost the altitude, and R3298 first flew with these (Hercules XI) in March 1942, Bristol having managed to squeeze the turbocharger into the existing cowling. However, the Hercules still proved so unsatisfactory at altitude that the production order for Mk Vs was switched to Mk VIs.

The Mk VI prototype W5795 first flew with Merlin 60 engines in November 1941, but despite the Merlin also having a two-stage two-speed supercharger, it was initially producing even less power than the Hercules VIII at high altitude, and further development was required, the aircraft ultimately reaching 37,000ft.

Early flights suffered a range of cold-related problems, such as jamming of control surfaces, jamming of bomb doors, and lumps of frozen oil damaging the structure; hence it was recommended that all hydraulic pipes be lagged and heated. Icing of the pilot's dome was a particular problem, and some flight tests ended with many minutes flying around at low altitude waiting for the view to clear, before a system was developed to pipe warm air to all the windows; two different dome shapes were used, and on some aircraft the dome could be lifted slightly at

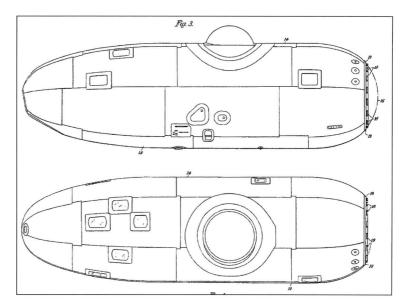

the front to allow the pilot to peek through, but this was not an ideal solution. Special fuel had to be used to prevent it boiling off under low pressure, and because of the higher fuel viscosity at low temperatures, fuel pumps were fitted to the wing tanks. Early test flights were conducted by 'Mutt' Summers (later joined by his brother Maurice and Tommy Lucke), and Jeffree flew on several flights between October 1940 and March 1941 to monitor the performance of the cabin pressure controller.

ABOVE Patent drawings of the pressure cabin of the Mk V and VI high-altitude Wellingtons. *(BAE Systems)*

BELOW W5795 was the Mk VI prototype retaining the longer nose fairing of the Mk V, seen here at Blackpool. This aircraft crashed in July 1942, the only pressure-cabin Wellington to be lost. The censor has obliterated the radio aerials on the hut in the background. *(Author's collection)*

To reach higher altitudes, extended wings were trialled on W5795 and W5800, 6ft extensions to each wingtip increasing wing area by 38sq ft. These increased the ceiling by only 200ft or so, and the extra curvature that they gave to the wings in flight was so alarming that they were removed again. Early aircraft had a long fairing beneath the pressure cabin, but this was made shorter on the production aircraft, giving the impression that the pressure cabin was further forward.

Throughout development, the inclusion of a rear turret remained contentious; some deemed it necessary (even if only for emergency use at lower altitudes), others as a waste of weight as the guns (and gunner) were unlikely to function reliably in the cold. Vickers studied a heated turret, and a partially pressurised FN.20 with heated guns was mocked-up, but further investigation favoured controlling the turret remotely from the pressure cabin with the navigator or wireless operator sighting using an underside periscope. Pending development of these ideas, it was decided to fix the rear guns astern, with the navigator firing them remotely, sighting by periscope, or the pilot firing them, sighting via a mirror in his dome and a bead attached to the fin.

Emergency exit from the pressure cabin was initially not straightforward. If the pilot could not descend quickly, the cabin had to be depressurised via an emergency valve, and once the pressure had equalised enough to open the door, the crew donned oxygen sets, collected parachutes from the fuselage and left via the entrance door (a personnel door added on the starboard side midway between the wing and tail). This procedure took at least 90 seconds. In the MK IV, the nose fairing beneath the pressure cabin was shortened to allow an emergency hatch to be fitted behind the bomb aimer's window. However, only one pressure-cabin aircraft crashed – in July 1942, a burst oil cooler caused prototype W5795 to shed a propeller blade and this punctured the pressure cabin, leading to instant decompression which would have incapacitated the crew, and the aircraft broke up as it fell to earth.

Two Mk VIs, DR480 and DR484, were given the Type 423 conversion to carry the 4,000lb HC bomb, 484 also, having its rear turret deleted and being fitted with Merlin 62s (with the undercarriage backstays extended further to balance).

At least 18 Mk VIGs were delivered with the Oboe blind-bombing aid in place of the bombsight, and at least four of these served with 109 Squadron; they were ultimately rejected in favour of the Mosquito for this role. Although 150 Mk VIs had initially been ordered, only 64 were built (all at VAX1) and they had all been struck off charge by the end of 1943. The experience gained with the pressure cabin, however, would be of value in designing later aircraft.

Test-bed Wellingtons

As a rugged aircraft with few vices, and in plentiful supply, the Wellington was pressed into service as a test-bed on many occasions, to be used for experiments with engines, armaments, and other systems.

'Bouncing Bomb' test-bed
Alongside his aircraft work, Wallis had also been developing some specialist bombs, one of which was to attack dams by skipping over the water to land alongside the wall. A range of model tests were conducted during 1942, and permission was given to convert a Wellington

BELOW The cockpit in the pressure cabin of a Mk V. *(BAE Systems via Brooklands Museum)*

for the dropping of larger test spheres, Mk III BJ895 being selected. Under Vickers Type 452, the bomb bay was converted to carry four of the 46in-diameter test bombs and, after ground spin tests, was flown on 2 December over a local reservoir by Summers to test handling with the bombs spinning. After modifications to carry only two bombs, the aircraft was flown on 4 December to Chesil Beach on the Dorset coast, again by Summers with Wallis as bomb aimer, and the two bombs were dropped for their first full test. At least six further tests were conducted during December and January, plus two drops over open sea in early March, before testing was moved to a new range at Reculver on the north Kent coast, the Wellington making at least three drops there before testing was taken over entirely by Mosquitoes and Lancasters.

BJ895 was converted back to standard specification and served with the Central Gunnery School at Leconfield in Yorkshire. In July 1946, it crashed near Scarborough while engaged in a fighter affiliation exercise.

Jet test beds

Three refurbished Wellington IIs were used to test Whittle jet engines, the first (Z8570) being allocated in April 1942 after consultation with Pierson on the feasibility of the installation. The jet engine was mounted in place of the rear turret of the aircraft, with the jet fuel being carried in bomb bay tanks, and a station was created in the fuselage for an engine operator with appropriate controls and instrumentation, including cameras to record the gauges. A Rover-built Whittle W.2B was fitted at Weybridge and ground tested during July, before transferring to the Rolls-Royce plant at Hucknall in Nottingham for the flight testing programme to begin the following month; Merlin XXs were subsequently substituted for the original Xs. Over the next year, several jet engines (and intake configurations) were tested on this aircraft, one engine exceeding 100 hours. Testing moved to a new facility at RAF Church Broughton in 1944 and continued until the aircraft was struck off charge in October 1945.

The success of the trials with Z8570 led to a request for more test aircraft. As their main function was to carry the test engines to their

ideal operating height, it was suggested that redundant Mk VIs be used for this, but the Rolls-Royce test pilots were not keen on the pressure cabin. One useful feature of the Mk VI was the inclusion of fuel pumps on the wing tanks, so two hybrid aircraft were created at Wisley using Mk IIs with the wings from Mk VIs – W5389 with DR524's wings and W5518 with W5802's wings (these were not the extended wings); Merlin 62s were also fitted. The noses were faired over (Z8570 had retained its nose turret) and improved mountings were used for the jet to make engine changes easier, W5518 also being used to test a 'thrust spoiler'. Both aircraft were used for tests with a variety of engines, accumulating 512 hours of operation over 366 flights and reaching 36,000ft. W5389 was scrapped in June 1947 and W5518 in March 1949.

Other engine test beds

Mk X LN715 was used to test the Rolls-Royce Dart turboprop installation intended for the Viscount, receiving the engines in place of its Hercules. After initial trials at Weybridge, the main test programme was conducted at Hucknall between 1948 and 1951. With the two Darts, the aircraft was actually underpowered at take-off, resulting in a long take-off run, but once up to operating height, performance was much better – and noticeably quieter than with the piston engines. NA857 was designated for similar trials with the Napier Naiad turboprop and it may have had these installed, although it appears that it never actually flew with them.

LN718 was used as a test bed for the Hercules 100 engine (with four-bladed propellers) to be used on the Viking.

Gun test beds

The machine-gun armament in British bombers was never a match for the cannon carried by German fighters, and there were many plans to fit more powerful defensive armament to bombers. One such weapon was trialled in Wellingtons – a Vickers 40mm cannon, known as the 'S' gun, the test bed being the Mk II prototype, L4250. This aircraft was fitted with a custom-designed turret mounted in the dorsal position just aft of the wing, the local fuselage structure being strengthened to support it. The turret carried the gunner, sighting apparatus, and a sophisticated predictor unit, which would automatically aim the gun as the gunner tracked a target in his sight. The first flight of the new turret experienced severe vibration, as the turret was disrupting the airflow over the fin, and the aircraft was modified to replace this with two fins mounted on the horizontal stabilisers. This proved satisfactory, although when the gun was test fired, the blast damaged the fabric covering on the wings. This aircraft was later used to trial another mid-upper turret carrying four 0.5in guns, before being scrapped. The 'S' gun was also tested in a nose installation in another Mk II, Z8416. The turret was faired over and the gun mounted in the extreme nose of the aircraft.

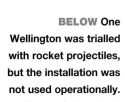

BELOW One Wellington was trialled with rocket projectiles, but the installation was not used operationally.
(Crown Copyright via The National Archives)

The gun could be depressed 5°, elevated 50°, and traversed 15° to each side, and was controlled by an operator in a retractable bubble canopy just behind the pilots. L4212, L4259 and L4329 were all used for tests of alternative turrets, including a dorsal turret, and there were proposals for many more which never reached the testing stage.

Rocket projectile test bed

In the summer of 1943, the Coastal Command Development Unit (CCDU) conducted trials with a Mk XIV (MP714) fitted with rocket projectiles, as used successfully by Beaufighters, Mosquitoes, and other aircraft. An 18SWG alloy plate was attached to the underside of the wing to protect the fabric, and two rails were fitted on either side of the fuel jettison pipe on each wing; a Mk IIIL reflector sight was fitted in the cockpit for aiming. Over 180 rockets with 25lb (anti-submarine) and 60lb (anti-shipping) warheads were fired on initial tests, and both aircraft handling and rocket performance were found to be satisfactory and no aircraft damage was incurred (although the pilots found it less suitable than other aircraft as an RP platform). Night trials against submarines using ASV Mk III and the Leigh Light were partly successful, but it was concluded that the usual load of depth charges was likely to be more successful in a real attack. It appears that the trials aircraft was the only one fitted with RPs and they were not used operationally.

Glider tugs

The Wellington was not an obvious choice as a glider tug as, even with the presence of the fuselage longerons, there was the possibility that the geodetics would tend to stretch in the manner of 'lazy tongs' under towing forces. Despite this, it was tested as a glider tug using a horseshoe-shaped towing bracket around the rear turret anchored to a tubular structure that passed through the fuselage forward of the rear turret through reinforced geodetics forward of the rear terminal ring; this was kept horizontal by a hydraulic damper. In the summer of 1942, Mk IC DV942 was tested at the Airborne Forces Experimental Establishment near Leeds with one and two Hotspurs, the

tests being principally to check that engine cooling was adequate, and the IC was deemed suitable for towing one, but not two, gliders. Mk III X3286 was tested with a Horsa the same year, and this aircraft and Mk X HE731 were tested with a Hadrian in the autumn, and both marks were cleared for operational use in both temperate and tropical climates, subject to minor modifications including the cropping of the engine gills to improve cooling. Warwick I BV230 was tested with a Hadrian and found to be satisfactory, though for temperate climates only. Wellington X9790 took part in 'Project SB22' towing a Hurricane in 1942, with a view to using this combination for ferrying fighters to Malta. Despite these generally positive tests, neither aircraft seems to have been used operationally as a glider tug, and opinion remains divided on how well the geodetic structure could have withstood prolonged service in this role.

Paratroop carriers

The usual method for exit of paratroops was to jump through a hole in the floor of the aircraft, and the Wellington had the perfect facility for this in the shape of the unused ventral turret fitting. There appears to have been no official paratroop door modification, but several field conversions were carried out – the turret hole was covered by two semi-circular inward-opening metal doors, and an external windshield added in front of the opening to reduce the tendency for the slipstream to push the parachutist into the rear of the opening before they had fallen clear of the aircraft. Ten paratroops could be carried, with four 350lb equipment containers in the bomb bay. Training drops were carried out, but no operational drops of paratroops are recorded.

Airborne interception

Driven initially by the need for long-range detection of Focke-Wulf FW200 Condor aircraft protecting the south-western approaches – but largely operating beyond the range of UK-based radar – an airborne detection solution was tested using Mk IC R1629. This was based on ASV Mk II but used a 15ft blade Yagi aerial mounted on a dorsal pylon; this aerial rotated at approximately 22rpm and

the system had a maximum detection range of 22 miles. It was evaluated in a series of trials from the Telecommunications Research Establishment at Defford from February 1942. Fighter Command was interested in its air interception potential, and it was used in 1944 for long-range detection of Heinkel He 111s deploying V1 flying bombs after their launch sites in France were captured. Although this use of air-controlled interception is now regarded as the forerunner to AWACS aircraft, it does not appear to have been widely deployed.

Other roles

The Wellington saw service in a variety of other specialist roles, often as one-offs, typically with conversions carried out by service personnel as required.

ABOVE Several Wellingtons (and a Warwick) were trialled as glider tugs using a yolk around the rear turret. Although cleared for operational use, the aircraft saw no service in this role. *(Crown Copyright via The National Archives)*

BELOW The ventral fitting converted into a paratroop door. *(Liam Venner/ www.214squadron.org.uk)*

ABOVE Some stills from *Workers' Week-end* show the bomber taking shape. *(Crown Copyright)*

THE '24-HOUR' WELLINGTON

With production of Wellingtons in full swing at all three Vickers factories, the Ministry of Information decided to use the aircraft as the subject of a propaganda newsreel, as a 'tribute to the workers of the British aircraft industry' and to boost Britons' spirits. The film would have the added excitement of documenting an attempt to assemble a complete Wellington Mk X in just 30 hours – breaking the existing construction record of 48 hours held by the Douglas Aircraft Company in California for a Boston (a twin-engined bomber of similar size and performance to the Wellington). As the film was also intended to appeal to the Allies, a narrator with North American accent was chosen for the film – 'an officer of the Royal Canadian Air Force', J. Peach.

Broughton was given the opportunity to go for the record, and the Crown Film Unit cameras arrived at the factory in the summer of 1943. Around 60 workers had given up their weekend off to take part, and were donating their overtime wages to charity – hence the film's title *Workers' Week-end*.

Work began on the aircraft on a Saturday morning (the exact date is not recorded), and followed the standard assembly procedure. The key times given in the film were as follows:

09:00 Construction starts with assembly of fuselage geodetic panels into jigs.

10:17 Wing assembly is in progress, cockpit seat assembly joined to fuselage.

10:27 Electrical fitting begins.

13:45 Fuselage removed from jig; wings being covered.

18:15 Fuselage mostly covered; engines attached; tail surfaces attached; bomb beam attached; fuel tanks inserted into outer wings and wings attached.

20:00 Night shift arrives.

20:23 Propellers are fitted; turrets are fitted.

22:23 Wheels are fitted; nacelle petrol tanks are fitted.

Sunday

03:00 Painting is nearing completion with roundels being painted (freehand!).

03:20 Inspections and engine tests begin.

06:15 Final engine tests, finishing touches to the covering.

08:50 The aircraft is readied for take-off, the pilot having to be woken early as they were ahead of schedule!

The aircraft took off 24 hours and 48 minutes after work began (smashing the record), and after making a few circuits to salute the workers, the film records that it was 'flown by a ferry pilot to its operational base' that evening. In fact, it appears that the aircraft – LN514 – went first (as most aircraft did) to a Maintenance Unit for final fitting out and a period of storage, later serving with 19 OTU, and it survived the war to be scrapped in 1948.

The film itself was commemorated in a 2010 BBC TV programme *Wellington Bomber*, which told the story of the aircraft and included interviews with some of those who had appeared in the original film.

Directional Wireless Installation – minesweeping from the air

In the autumn of 1939, the Germans began to air-drop a new type of sea mine that appeared able to detonate without physical contact with a ship. It was suspected that the mines might be triggered acoustically or magnetically, and the latter was confirmed when one was dropped on mudflats and successfully defused on 23 November by two Royal Navy mine countermeasures officers. The mechanism was found to be activated by a magnetic needle moving under the influence of a passing ship.

Finding a way to defeat this new menace became a top priority, and the 'boffins' proposed a number of options, from the bizarre – such as attaching powerful bar magnets to fish and releasing them in mined areas – to more practical solutions using aircraft. It was suggested that an aircraft carrying a powerful electromagnet might be able to trigger the mines if flying low overhead – assuming it could avoid the explosion should it succeed!

Bar electromagnets were found not to be powerful enough, but Wallis, in conjunction with the Admiralty Research Laboratory, designed a 48ft hoop coil that could be carried by a Wellington or a Harrow (other aircraft were also considered initially), powered by a motor-driven generator inside the fuselage. However, wind tunnel tests showed that the Harrow would be unstable carrying the coil, so only the Wellington was proceeded with – and the task was of such urgency that Churchill demanded that a progress report, with photographs, be sent to him every 24 hours.

A large, spindly turntable was constructed in one corner of the Weybridge factory, upon which the coil was wound – aluminium was chosen as it offered the best compromise between magnetic performance and coil weight, and a single strip 2in x 0.226in x 9,650ft long was wound into 64 turns in the manner of a clock

BELOW The principle of the DWI installation, to scale for an aircraft flying at 30ft over a mine 30ft deep. The red arrow shows the magnetic force which triggers the mine. *(Author)*

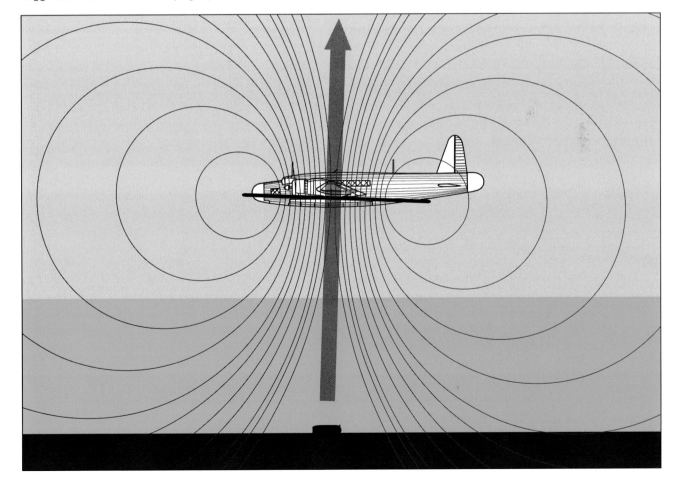

spring, with impregnated cotton tape being fed in between the turns to insulate each from its neighbours. The finished coil was enclosed in an aerodynamic shell made from balsa wood bound with tape; small air intakes at the front and sides forced air through the casing to cool the coil.

The first coil was completed at Weybridge on 19 December, and the empty casing was test flown on Wellington Mk I P2518 two days later. The front turret was replaced by a fairing to which the coil was attached, and the rear turret was also removed to save weight, as were all turret hydraulics, bomb gear, bomb aimer's window, and the rear row of wing fuel tanks (though the bomb beam was retained to support the generating equipment above the bomb bay roof). The coil was also attached below the rear fuselage by a wooden frame at station 72 and at the wings via tubular fittings to the lower main spar booms. The installation was completed on 28 December (work had continued right through Christmas), although because of bad weather the first flight was not until two days later. Aircraft handling was found to be close to normal (but the compass was rendered useless – a gyro compass was fitted later); the aircraft AUW was 27,700lb with 416 gallons of fuel, and it required an 800yd

take-off run using no flap (the inboard flaps had been disconnected and bolted shut to avoid aerodynamic interference with the coil).

To energise the coil, a 35kW Mawdsley generator driven by a Ford V8 engine was mounted on wooden runners in the central fuselage, the redundant frames for the ventral turret being used to install this equipment via a block and tackle. This combination produced 310 amps at 110 volts, giving 19,800-ampere turns generating a magnetic field of 0.47 gauss – enough to trigger a mine less than 120ft away. The generator was sited immediately abaft the main spar, and the engine between that and the trailing edge frame; fuel for the engine came from the port nacelle tank. The engine had no external air intake, but cooling was provided for the exhaust, and a control panel was fitted on the port side ahead of the main spar for the operator who had a hot, noisy job beside the plant – the pilot had no controls for the equipment. The engine oil and generator coil temperatures had to be closely monitored and the plant shut down if either became too hot (which they often did); the coil resistance increased as it heated up, reducing the current and hence the strength of the magnetic field. At A&AEE Boscombe Down, the prototype was

repeatedly flown over the mechanism recovered from the German mine, at a variety of heights and sideways displacements, to test the ability of the coil to trigger the mechanism.

Four Mk IAs were initially converted, coils for all four being made by Experimental Department staff at Weybridge under George Edwards. After preliminary testing, it was decided to increase the strength of the output, so staff at the RAE redesigned the coil using a thinner but longer strip 1.6in x 0.085in x 23,000ft long giving 152 turns. This was energised by a converted English Electric trolley bus motor driven by a DH Gipsy Six aero-engine producing 200 amps at 450 volts, giving 30,040-ampere turns and a consequent increase in magnetic field strength of around 50%, which meant that the aircraft did not have to fly so low. As the new generating plant was 700lb lighter (the coil weighed about the same), this allowed more fuel to be carried, giving greater endurance.

This new combination first flew on 2 March and was designated DWI Mk II (Vickers Type 419), the four Mk I aircraft (Type 418) being subsequently converted to the Mk II standard. The English Electric Company fabricated the Mk II coils. They were fitted with casings made by Briggs Motor Bodies, and assembled and fitted

ABOVE The Ford V8 engine and Mawdsley generator used in the DWI Mk I. *(RAF Museum)*

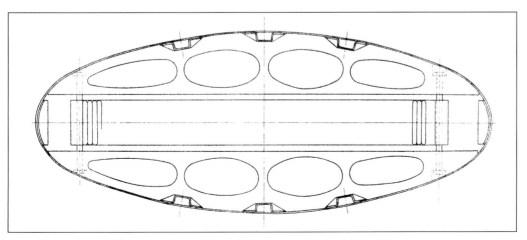

LEFT Cross-section of the DWI Mk I coil showing the 64 turns and the frame of the aerodynamic shell. *(Crown Copyright via The National Archives)*

by Rollason Aircraft Services of Croydon. Twelve Mk IIs were flown in addition to the four Mk Is.

It was realised that DWI would only succeed if the aircraft could avoid the plume of water thrown up by any mines exploded by the apparatus. The Admiralty Research Laboratories filmed detonations of 1,500lb charges in water between 30ft and 90ft deep to record the formation and rate of growth of the plume, and hence calculated the safety margins for various speed and height combinations. For the preferred sweep height of 30ft, this gave a 36ft safety margin from a mine at a depth of 90ft when flying at 100mph, or 60ft at 140mph. The latter was deemed the minimum safe speed, and if the water was shallow, initial sweeps were to be made at a greater height to preserve the safety margin. Increased aircraft speed also reduced the effect of the magnetic impulse on the mine, so that it took longer to operate, meaning that the aircraft was further away when it exploded (although in off-track cases, the reduced impulse might not be enough to detonate the mine at all). The width of the swept channel was proportional to aircraft height, being around 90ft wide at a depth of 60ft when flying at 30ft and 140mph.

DWI in operation

No 1 General Reconnaissance Unit (GRU) of Coastal Command was formed at RAF Manston on 19 December under Sqn Ldr John Chaplin 'for the purpose of magnetic mine sweeping' principally in the Thames Estuary. The GRU's first operational sweeps were made using P2518 on 9 January 1940, accompanied by Hurricane escorts and two Ansons on photographic duties; lightships and MTBs were used as markers in an attempt to sweep accurate channels. The first mine was successfully exploded on 13 January, with the second later the same day (the blasts registering 3g and 10g respectively on on-board instruments) and, by the end of February, a further three aircraft were also in operation (P2521, P2522 and P9223). The Mk II aircraft began to arrive early in March, and the Mk I aircraft were dispatched to Croydon to be upgraded.

A second GRU was formed at Bircham Newton in Norfolk on 4 March, and as it began to receive DWI aircraft, joined in on sweeps

off the east coast. In addition to single aircraft sweeps, dual sweeps were also used, and a triple sweep was attempted for the first time on 21 March – this was more effective than three single aircraft, but required tight formation flying at low level. By the end of the month, a total of 14 mines had been exploded – almost certainly saving 14 ships from severe damage or worse. Sweeps continued through April and into May, including performing sweeps off IJmuiden in Holland in advance of the departure of the Dutch Royal Family to Britain.

Another GRU was formed at Manston at the end of April, but a month later it moved to Thorney Island in West Sussex to protect the approaches to Portsmouth. However, a new type of mine was deployed in the summer of 1940 and this was found to be virtually immune to aerial sweeping as the magnetic impulse needed to be applied for a much longer time, so No 3 GRU was disbanded at the end of July, although ship-based minesweeping continued, assisted by the development of degaussing techniques to reduce the magnetic signature of ships.

Meanwhile, the perceived threat to the Suez Canal resulted in No 2 GRU being merged into No 1 and the unit being sent to Egypt. With the heavy coil and generating plant aboard, the Wellington had insufficient range to make the hops to Egypt, so Rollason's were employed again to strip the equipment from the aircraft, so that it could be sent by sea. The first five aircraft (L4227, L4235, L4374, L4391, and L7771) left Britain on 20 May, although L4391 crashed during take-off from one of the refuelling stops and was beyond repair. Reunited with their equipment at Ismailia, near the mid-point of the canal, three of the DWI aircraft were operational by 11 June, with the fourth ready a week later, and work was started immediately sweeping the harbour at Alexandria and the canal itself. The heat and dust caused some cooling problems for the coils (which had larger air scoops fitted) and also for the aircraft. The unit's own maintenance crews performed sterling work keeping the aircraft operational, and despite an ongoing shortage of parts (including dope for the covering) they performed major overhauls, including refitting engines, replacing fabric, and changing coils if necessary. P2518 and L4356 arrived from the UK in July 1941, and this allowed three or four aircraft to be kept operational most of the time, even during repairs and refits. The DWI Wellingtons were unarmed (other than a single Browning carried by some in the astro-hatch), but a number had their nose and tail fairings painted to look like turrets, complete with wooden 'guns'.

Throughout 1940 and into 1941, sweeps continued to be made and mines were exploded from time to time. In January 1942, L4374 was lost while being used on radar calibration duties – an engine failed out over the Mediterranean, and although not carrying a coil, the weight of the generator plant meant it lost height rapidly and ditched with the loss of the crew. Sweeps of the canal were made every three or four days during 1942 and, in November, some of the aircraft were detached to sweep the recaptured harbours at Tobruk, Benghazi, and Tripoli. In April 1943, HX682 arrived at Ismailia, becoming the final Wellington to be converted to DWI – it was also the only Mk IC conversion and the only aircraft to be converted 'in the field'. Sweeping continued on several days each month during 1943 and early 1944, but in March the GRU was disbanded. The aircraft were transferred to 162 Squadron based at Idku near Alexandria, which continued to operate them as required until July when the squadron was itself disbanded, and the remaining DWIs (L4356, L4358, L7771, and HX682) were scrapped. A total of 39 mines are believed to have been exploded by DWI operations.

Some of the DWIs that were retained in the UK were converted for other duties. These included P9223, which was used for Leigh Light trials, and P2521, which flew with 161 Squadron as an 'airborne telephone exchange' flying over the French coast to relay messages to and from SIS field agents.

Summary

With more than 9,000 bombers and 2,000 other variants produced, Wellington manufacture exceeded every other multi-engined British aircraft of the war, and it was used in a greater variety of roles than any other large aircraft. On average, more than 120 Wellingtons were produced each month between 1938 and 1945.

Between 1911 and 1970, just over 16,000 aircraft were built under the Vickers name, and it is remarkable to note that the 11,462 Wellingtons and 846 Warwicks built between 1937 and 1946 make up more than 75% of this total. Both shadow factories each produced more aircraft than Weybridge (even including Warwicks).

The Wellington had shown geodetics to be superior to contemporary construction alternatives, but the advent of jet travel, with its greater speeds and heights, meant that it had become outdated. However, the Wellington was 'the right plane at the right time' and its contribution to the war and beyond is difficult to overstate.

Aircraft v. Magnetic Mine

"Wellingtons were fitted with a device for exploding the magnetic mines laid by the enemy in our waters."

"The Wellington was soon found to be the aircraft most suited to the purpose, and a number were equipped with a hoop-shaped casing extending all round them and secured to their nose, wings and tail."
Coastal Command, 1939–42.

VICKERS-ARMSTRONGS
LIMITED
WEYBRIDGE WORKS

ABOVE By 1944, DWI was no longer secret and was being used in advertising. *(BAE Systems)*

Chapter Two

The Wellington at War

━━━●━━━

The Wellington was the mainstay of Bomber Command during the first few years of the war, until the arrival of the next generation of four-engined bombers. It was extensively used by Coastal Command as a U-boat hunter by day and night, and was the backbone of Operational Training Units. It was widely used in the Mediterranean and Middle East, and also saw service in the Far East and with several Allied air forces.

OPPOSITE A Mk XIII dropping supplies over Greece. Note the ASV Mk II 'stickleback' aerials, a covered beam window and unarmed rear turret. The block under the nose is an F.46 camera for recording torpedo drops. *(IWM TR2805)*

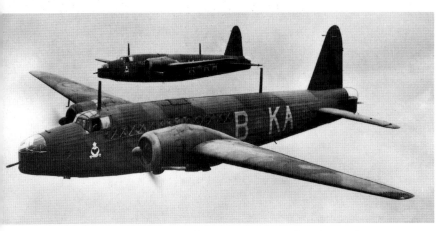

ABOVE Classic pre-war shot of Mk I Wellingtons, with the 9 Squadron badge beneath the cockpit; note the other features unique to this mark, such as the Vickers turrets, double aerial masts and sliding astro-hatch. *(Author's collection)*

Service with Bomber Command

As the rise of Nazism in Germany was watched with increasing concern in the early 1930s, Britain debated what level of military response was required. When rearmament was begun in earnest in the middle of the decade, it was the latest aircraft available at that time that were destined to protect Britain from invasion and to take the war to Germany.

The RAF's designs from the early part of the decade, such as the Harrow, Hendon, Battle, and Wellesley, were recognised as obsolescent even as they went into service, and the Blenheim, Whitley, Hampden, and

Wellington began to replace them just in time to see service for a few months before the war began. The first Wellington was received by 99 Squadron in October 1938, with five more squadrons receiving them within six months, and ten Bomber Command squadrons had them by the outbreak of war. This allowed some 'war game' exercises to be undertaken in the summer of 1939, as well as some 'flag-waving' excursions to Europe.

The new generation of aircraft was designed, and their crews trained, for daylight bombing – with pinpoint military and industrial targets in Germany able to be struck with ease if propaganda, and some RAF leaders, were to be believed. However, although the latest bombers were up to the job in theory, the truth was far from this ideal, with navigation and bomb aiming both primitive and heavily dependent on good weather.

Armed Hampdens and Wellingtons were both in the air on the first day of the war, looking for enemy shipping, but no contact was made. Blenheims and Wellingtons attacked shipping on 4 September, both forces losing aircraft, although 55 Wellington 'North Sea sweep' sorties were flown over the next two months with no loss. Attacks on naval targets in December (see Chapter 5) resulted in 25% losses for

RIGHT The Bristol Blenheim continued in the daylight bombing role after other aircraft had switched to night bombing, and suffered accordingly. This is a Mk IV. *(Jonathan Falconer collection)*

the Wellington force – mostly from fighter attack (although staff officers were reluctant to believe this). As a result, particularly following the notorious 'Battle of Heligoland Bight' on 18 December, Bomber Command decided to switch to night bombing (although daylight attacks, especially by Blenheims in the ground support role, continued until the fall of France). This policy initially reduced combat losses, but it also exacerbated the problems of navigation and bomb aiming, and it was not uncommon for aircraft to drop bombs many miles off target. Early Wellington combat experience also led to the fitting of self-sealing fuel tanks and more armour plating, and the poorly armed Mk Is were replaced by IAs from November.

Early 1940 saw RAF operations in support of the Norwegians, and the start of minelaying operations (known as 'gardening'), although this was done almost exclusively by Hampdens, with Wellingtons participating occasionally from August. Germany invaded the Low Countries and France in May, and tactical support of the

British Expeditionary Force was given. After the evacuation from Dunkirk, the strategic bombing offensive moved on to Germany itself, with occasional targets in Italy, which had joined the Axis in June. Attention was also given to barges in the Channel ports and other targets associated with a German build-up for an invasion of Britain. When Sir Richard Peirse became AOC Bomber Command in October, he had at his disposal around 100 Wellingtons from a force of about 230 aircraft; these were usually sent out individually to find their own way to their targets.

Along with Mk ICs, the first Merlin-engined Mk IIs and Hercules-engined Mk IIIs began to reach squadrons over the winter, and the new 4,000lb 'Cookie' was first dropped on Emden

BELOW The nose
of 'R for Robert',
showing the geodetic
construction to best
advantage. The slots
in the wing's leading
edge are air intakes
for the cabin heating
system. *(Author)*

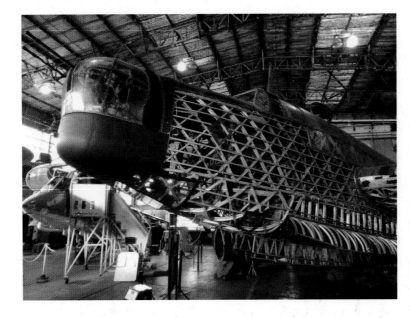

by a Mk II of 149 Squadron on the night of 31 March 1941. However, German nightfighter strength was also increasing, and these had developed the tactic of creeping up astern of their target where the tail gunner, even if he saw the attacker, was outgunned – as a result, bomber losses during 1941 were ten times as great as 1940.

The Wellington force continued to grow, both in size and proportion, and by November the aircraft formed over 40% of Bomber Command's front-line strength, reaching a peak of 25 operational squadrons in January 1942. When Arthur Harris took over from Peirse the following month, he wanted to demonstrate the power of his Command and staged three 'Thousand Bomber' raids. The first of these, at the end of May 1942, saw just over 1,000 aircraft sent to Cologne, of which 60% were Wellingtons, more than 200 of which were drafted in from OTUs to reach the desired total. The Wellington contingents of the other two raids, to Essen on 1 June and Bremen on 25 June, were 57% and 44% respectively.

Harris was also keen to accelerate the introduction of the new four-engined heavy bombers, and as these arrived, the Wellington began to be phased out – although more slowly than the Blenheim, Hampden, and Whitley (which was retired within a few months). It is notable, however, that the ultimate bomber variant, the Mk X, only started production in the summer of 1942, and the Wellington's production run was only halfway through at this time.

The last major Bomber Command raid in which the Wellington took part as a bomber was on 8 October 1943, although it remained in use for minor operations such as minelaying, and continued in the ELINT role into 1945. OTUs also continued to dispatch Wellingtons on 'nickel' operations.

JAMES ALLEN WARD VC

On 7 July 1941, 49 Wellingtons were dispatched on a raid to Münster. Returning over the IJsselmeer, a 75 (New Zealand) Squadron aircraft (L7818, one of the first batch of Mk ICs) was attacked from beneath by a Messerschmitt Bf 110 nightfighter, damaging the hydraulics and the inner starboard wing, which was set on fire, fed by a leaking petrol line. After unsuccessful attempts to douse the fire from inside the fuselage, the second pilot, Sergeant James Allen Ward volunteered to attempt to smother the fire with an engine cover that was stored in the fuselage. Using the rope from the dinghy as a safety line, he climbed out of the astrodome then, donning his parachute (which he had reluctantly been persuaded to take by the navigator) he was able to climb down the fuselage and clamber along the wing to the fire, kicking holes in the fabric covering to create hand- and foot-holds as he went – the slipstream threatening to blow him off at any time, even though the pilot had reduced to minimum flying speed. Ward managed to smother the fire with the engine cover, and pushed it into the hole, but it was quickly blown out again. However, with the fire out, the aircraft was out of immediate danger, and he climbed back into the aircraft with the navigator's assistance. The Canadian pilot, Sqn Ldr Reuben Widdowson, managed to make an emergency landing at Newmarket, despite the damage to the aircraft, which was so bad that it never flew again.

For his actions in saving the aircraft and crew, Ward was recommended for a Victoria Cross, the highest military bravery award. The shy, quiet pilot was overwhelmed by the honour and the publicity that surrounded it, including meeting Prime Minister Winston Churchill.

Given his own command, Ward continued to fly with 75 Squadron, but on 15 September, on his fifth operation in command, his aircraft was hit by flak over Hamburg and crashed. Only two of the crew survived, and Ward is now buried in the Commonwealth War Graves Commission plot in Hamburg's main cemetery. A hall at his former college in New Zealand and a community centre (formerly the Sergeants' Mess) at RAF Feltwell in Norfolk, where 75 Squadron were based, are now both named in his honour.

Ward was the only person to be awarded

LEFT James Allen Ward VC demonstrates the outward opening cockpit roof windows. He was the only recipient of a VC for action in a Wellington. *(Imperial War Museum)*

a VC for action in a Wellington, out of 31 VCs awarded to airmen of the UK and Commonwealth air forces. His medal is currently on display in the Auckland War Memorial Museum.

BELOW Close-up of the damage caused to Vickers Wellington Mark IC, L7818 'AA-V', of No 75 (New Zealand) Squadron RAF, at Feltwell, Norfolk, after returning from an attack on Münster, Germany, on the night of 7/8 July 1941. While over the IJsselmeer, cannon shells from an attacking Messerschmitt Bf 110 struck the starboard wing (A), causing a fire from a fractured fuel line which threatened to spread to the whole wing. Efforts by the crew to douse the flames failed, and Sergeant James Allen Ward, the second pilot, volunteered to tackle the fire by climbing out on to the wing via the astro-hatch (B). With a dinghy-rope tied around his waist, he made hand- and foot-holds in the fuselage and wings (1, 2 and 3) and moved out across the wing from where he was eventually able to extinguish the burning wing-fabric. His courageous actions earned him the Victoria Cross. *(IWM CH3223)*

WERE YOU MORE LIKELY TO RETURN IN A WELLINGTON?

The Wellington acquired (and has maintained) a remarkable reputation that it could 'get you home' from a mission, even though badly shot up, this often being attributed to its geodetic construction. This case is often supported by photographs of flak-damaged Wellingtons with large parts of the fabric covering burnt or torn away, exposing the geodetics beneath … sometimes with large holes in the structure itself. Part of the reason that Wellingtons could survive this kind of damage is down to the fact that the geodetics occupied a relatively small part of the surface – whereas a hole in a stressed-skin panel might weaken it substantially, a hole in the fabric skin of a Wellington might miss the structure altogether. Even if the geodetics *were* damaged, the redundancy inherent in the structure meant that it could survive the loss of some members, whereas a stressed-skin structure might tear open and fail completely. However, other aircraft did limp home with serious damage too, so is the Wellington's reputation truly deserved?

It is quite difficult to make a meaningful comparison with the Wellington's contemporaries for several reasons: different aircraft served during different periods of the war, different aircraft were used for different duties, and the way that statistics were gathered about operational losses changed throughout the war, so that even raw data are not always comparable. Later marks would have returned more frequently, as the Wellington could maintain height on one Hercules, but not on one Pegasus (at least 'on paper', although some did make it home after judicious lightening of the aircraft).

Table 1 shows the loss figures over the whole war for the principal British aircraft types serving with Bomber Command. It can be seen that the Wellington has the lowest loss rate of its contemporaries, and is the best of the two-engined aircraft except for the fast, high-flying Mosquito.

It is perhaps more useful to examine just the

BELOW A well-known cartoon extolling the virtues of the Wellington's resilience to damage. *(Author's collection)*

"ONLY ANOTHER THOUSAND MILES CHARLIE, AND WE'LL BE HOME." FREDDIE.

Service in the Middle East

Although the RAF had 20 squadrons in the Middle East in September 1939, they all had obsolescent aircraft, and the region was given low priority for re-equipping. The first Wellingtons to reach the region were special-duty DWI aircraft in May 1940, but the first bomber aircraft did not arrive at the incumbent 70 Squadron until September, immediately being put to use in regular attacks on Benghazi. Nos 37, 38 and 148 Squadrons were transferred from Bomber Command and flown to Egypt, taking part in some bombing raids on Italy and western Libya from Malta en route, then assisting with Operation Compass pushing west from Egypt into Libya. Some of these aircraft were sent to Greece, following the Italian invasion in October, but were withdrawn again when German forces joined this campaign. As the North African campaign ebbed and flowed, the squadrons saw repeated changes of base, and ground crews performed miracles keeping the aircraft flying in harsh conditions (especially sand) and often with little outside logistical support – fabric and dope for the covering were particularly difficult to keep 'in stock'.

In 1941, the Royal Navy's Fleet Torpedo Officer, Commander Watson, was looking for a long-range torpedo bomber to attack Rommel's supply convoys. Lt Ben Bolt (who had been naval representative on DWI) suggested converting a Wellington – he knew that John Chaplin (an ex-DWI pilot) was CO of 38 Squadron at Shallufa, so Watson sent

OPPOSITE Vickers Wellington Mark ICs of 37 Squadron being prepared for a raid at an Advanced Landing Ground, probably LG09/Bir Koraiyim in Egypt, during bombing operations against Italian ports and airfields in Libya. Groundcrew are about to refuel T2508 'LF-O', which has just had its port main wheel replaced after bursting a tyre on landing. *(IWM CM368)*

Aircraft	Sorties	Lost	as %
Mosquito	39,795	310	0.78
Lancaster	156,192	3,677	2.35
Halifax	82,773	2,083	2.52
Wellington	47,409	1,727	3.64
Stirling	18,440	684	3.71
Hampden	16,541	633	3.83
Blenheim	12,214	541	4.43
Whitley	9,858	458	4.65
Manchester	1,269	76	5.99

Table 1
Losses by aircraft type (data from
***The Bomber Command War Diaries*)**

actually fared *worse* than the Hampden over the next 22 months (although the Whitley was the worst of the three, and it was withdrawn from front-line service after this period). Note that from June 1940 the *War Diaries* do not always give the number of each *type* of aircraft being dispatched, so the data shown cover only those raids where data for sorties and losses made by particular types *is* available.

The *War Diaries* indicate that the Hampden's loss rate on minelaying operations is virtually identical to that from bombing operations, so although minelaying operations were carried out almost exclusively by Hampdens up to 1942, this does not affect the figures.

In summary (for aircraft flying with Bomber Command), although a Wellington was more likely to get you home than a Hampden or Whitley on average over the whole war, the Hampden actually appears to have been the safest of the three for the period up to spring 1942.

early war period – losses up to April 1942 are listed in Table 2. This shows that the Wellington suffered more than the Hampden during daylight raids over the first nine months of the war, and the aircraft had similar losses from night raids over the same period; the Wellington then

	Wellington			Hampden			Whitley		
	Sorties	Lost	as %	Sorties	Lost	as %	Sorties	Lost	as %
Daylight bombing 3 Sep 1939 to 25 Jun 1940	365	27	7.4	247	17	6.9	32	0	0.0
Night bombing and minelaying 3 Sep 1939 to 25 Jun 1940	1,401	22	1.6	1,674	26	1.6	1,472	35	2.4
Night bombing and minelaying 26 Jun 1940 to 26 Apr 1942	14,026	391	2.8	8,000	194	2.4	4,016	149	3.7

Table 2
Losses up to 26 Apr 1942 for three aircraft types (data derived from *The Bomber Command War Diaries*)

ABOVE Early Mk XIIIs
of 38 Squadron at a
Mediterranean base in
1944. No 38 Squadron
flew Wellingtons
throughout the war.
(Author's collection)

his deputy, M.C. Morgan-Giles to 'sit on their doorstep and drink their gin until they let you try it'. However, Chaplin was very welcoming and a Wellington with two 2,000lb bomb beams had its bomb doors removed to carry two standard Mk XII torpedoes in the outer bomb cells. Initial trials in December dropped dummy torpedoes into the sand at Shallufa, then torpedoes with dummy warheads into the Gulf of Suez. Night trials followed, flying up the Moon path to help judge height, but on one flight a wingtip hit the water and the aircraft crashed, sinking immediately. Morgan-Giles had been acting as observer and was lucky to escape; half of the crew did not. Tactics were developed over the next few months – 221 Squadron flying Mk VIIIs with ASV would drop flares to illuminate targets, then the 38 Squadron Mk IC aircraft, using the flares or moonlight to silhouette the ships, would fly in at 70–80ft to drop their torpedoes. The first ship was sunk on 27 March 1942, but missions from Egypt were up to ten hours, requiring overload fuel tanks to be carried, and the squadrons eventually moved to Malta. AD646 was similarly converted for formal trials at the Torpedo Development Unit at Gosport, and the conversion was subsequently fitted to new Mk VIII, XI and XIII aircraft.

Later aircraft had only the rearmost set of bomb doors removed, to clear the 4ft-wide air tails on the torpedoes; these tails were wide enough to interfere with each other so either one torpedo was carried slightly ahead of the other, or one torpedo was carried nose-down

and one nose-up so the tails overlapped safely. Ultimately, the air tails were removed and the torpedoes carried wholly internally.

Once Rommel was defeated in North Africa in early 1943, Wellington operations switched to conventional bombing missions to Italy from North Africa and Malta. Following the landings at Anzio, bases in Italy itself were used up to March 1945 for missions including attacks on German forces in Yugoslavia and mining of the River Danube.

Wellingtons also saw limited service in Iraq, Syria, Palestine, and other Middle East countries, taking part in front-line operations into 1945.

Service in the Far East

The supply of bomber aircraft to the Far East was even more restricted than to the Middle East, and it was 1942 before the first Wellingtons, of 99 and 215 Squadrons, were dispatched to India. Staging through the Middle East, some of the Mk ICs and IIIs were pressed into service along the way, and it was the end of April before the first squadron was ready for operations from Pandaveswar in Bengal, eastern India. From there, they flew mostly long-range night bombing missions over Japanese-occupied Burma, to disrupt communications and supply lines and prevent forces reaching India. Conditions were harsh, with mountainous terrain to negotiate and tropical weather systems giving unpredictable winds and often icing conditions shortly after leaving scorching temperatures on the ground. Aircrew were also aware that any forced landing in the dense jungle was likely to be unpleasant, as was their treatment if captured by Japanese forces.

These two squadrons were the only ones to operate Wellingtons in India in 1942–43, and in May 1943, moved further east to Jessore (now in Bangladesh). They became part of Air Command South East Asia under Sir Richard Peirse when it was formed in November 1943, as did 8 and 244 Squadrons based in the Arabian peninsula, and 203 and 621 Squadrons which moved from Africa to Santacruz, Bombay (now Mumbai) and Aden (now Yemen) respectively. All four were engaged in maritime reconnaissance of the northern Indian Ocean using Wellington XIIIs.

No 99 Squadron had been flying Mk Xs and made the last Wellington bombing sortie over Burma in August 1944, being replaced by Liberators. The squadron was then switched to the transport role using Mk XVIs, and by May 1945 only 621 Squadron remained operational with Wellingtons in the region.

Service with Coastal Command

Coastal Command was formed in 1936 as the RAF's maritime arm and, during the war, was primarily concerned with U-boat warfare for convoy protection, also undertaking anti-shipping, air-sea rescue, and reconnaissance (especially meteorological) duties. Always given lower priority than Fighter and Bomber Commands, Coastal Command began the war poorly equipped with obsolescent aircraft of limited range (the few Sunderland flying boats available being their only adequate aircraft), and with few weapons suitable for attacking U-boats. During the early war years, the situation gradually improved, particularly with the development of the 250lb Torpex-filled depth charge and ASV radar, and as Whitleys and Wellingtons were superseded in Bomber Command, these aircraft were transferred for further duty with Coastal Command, which eventually started to receive new-build aircraft. Initially, Coastal Command Wellingtons retained the standard night bomber

ABOVE Armourers check a mixed load of 250lb HE and Small Bomb Containers (SBC) filled with 4lb incendiaries in the bomb bay of a Wellington Mk X of No 99 Squadron at Jessore, India, prior to a sortie over Burma. Note the downward-pointing F.24 target camera at the top right. *(IWM CF135)*

camouflage, but later the black was replaced by white, later still the green/brown upper surfaces were replaced by sea grey.

With no definite targets, patrol duration was determined by the Prudent Limit of Endurance, the point at which the pilot believed he could get back to base with an adequate margin of fuel remaining – if the weather, the enemy and his aircraft all obliged. The area covered on patrol was thus related to both the range and speed of the aircraft, and the Wellington's substantial range (especially with overload fuel tanks) meant that it was better suited to this task than many contemporary types, and its bomb bay could carry up to six 250lb depth charges.

The problem of detection persisted, as U-boats tended to remain submerged during the day, only surfacing under cover of darkness to ventilate and recharge their batteries. ASV gradually took over from visual observation as the main means of detecting U-boats, especially as its range was extended (up to about seven miles, further for larger targets), and of course it also worked at night. However, reflections from the sea surface cluttered the short-range part of the ASV display – hence, while the radar could guide an aircraft towards a surface target, its close-in accuracy was not good enough for timing the release of weapons – and it was also highly desirable to make a visual identification before attacking a target, which might be a fishing vessel rather than a U-boat. These substantial difficulties meant that Coastal

Command aircraft sank only two U-boats in the year up to May 1942.

Some method of illuminating targets was thus required, and two methods were trialled using Wellingtons. The first was the Turbinlite, which had originally been developed by William Helmore and Frederick Cotton to combat night bombers – Douglas Havoc aircraft had been fitted with powerful battery-powered searchlights in their noses, and used Airborne Interception (AI) radar (from which ASV had been developed) to detect enemy aircraft which were then illuminated with the Turbinlite, to permit accompanying nightfighters to attack. However, it was found to be impractical and was quickly superseded by better nightfighters carrying their own AI radar for locating their own targets. Wellington T2977, a Mk VIII with ASV Mk II, was fitted with a Turbinlite in its nose for trials at the CCDU at RAF Carew Cheriton in Pembrokeshire.

The second searchlight system was developed by Wg Cdr Humphrey de Verd 'Sammy' Leigh, a First World War pilot who was now an RAF Administration Officer. Originally designed with the light inside the fuselage shining on to a mirror lowered beneath the aircraft, it was decided to exploit the Wellington's unused ventral position, utilising the turret mechanism to lower the searchlight itself below the aircraft's belly. The trials aircraft selected was P9223, a redundant DWI aircraft that retained its generating plant, and which could be used to power the searchlight, the designation DWI Mk III initially being used for the project. The CCDU trials favoured the Leigh Light, and Mk VIII aircraft began to be fitted with the device, the trials unit No 1417 Flight being renamed 172 Squadron when it became operational from RAF Chivenor in Devon in April 1942. To maintain a greater level of alertness during long patrols, three wireless operators/air gunners were typically carried – they manned the radio, rear turret, and ASV station, changing places every 20 minutes or so. Because of the secret nature of the apparatus, aircrews were told not to bale out over enemy territory in an emergency, but to ditch their aircraft in deep water.

The system had an early first success – on 4 June, Sqn Ldr J.H. Greswell (who had taken part in the trials) picked up an ASV contact in the southern Bay of Biscay at six miles and carried out a textbook attack; the Italian submarine *Luigi Torelli* was illuminated and straddled with a stick of depth charges, although it managed to limp back to port. U-boats would have had lookouts posted when on the surface, but noise from the diesel engines and the sea meant that approaching aircraft could not be heard, and the sudden appearance of a Leigh Light aircraft bearing down from less than a mile distant would have come as a shock to the submarine crews. Before the end of June, further unsuccessful attacks had so unsettled Admiral Dönitz (the German commander of submarines) that he ordered his U-boats to stay submerged at night, preferring them to risk attack in daylight, when incoming aircraft could at least be seen.

A miniature 'arms race' then ensued between Coastal Command and the Kriegsmarine, each side briefly managing to gain the upper hand before the other side developed countermeasures.

By August 1942 the Germans had developed a radar detector (Metox), which was sensitive to ASV Mk II wavelengths. As this could detect ASV at twice the range at which the ASV aircraft could receive radar echoes, it was able to give a U-boat sufficient time to crash dive before the aircraft detected it. Suspecting that the Germans had such a detector even before they actually did, Coastal Command used two tactics – one was only to switch on the ASV for ten seconds every fifteen minutes, and the other was to have many aircraft fly higher than usual (up to 15,000ft) with their ASV on in an attempt to flood the sky with ASV signals, hence creating many false alarms and prevent the U-boats from discriminating between the flooding signals and an imminent attack. The U-boats had tricks of their own, such as Aphrodite – this was a raft to which a balloon was attached by a cable carrying three metal foil strips. These would reflect radar and hence act as a decoy to fool ASV operators into homing on to the Aphrodite while the U-boat made good its escape.

Coastal Command's next major innovation was ASV Mk III, developed from the H2S terrain radar which entered service with Bomber

LEIGH LIGHT PROCEDURE

Normal search height is 1,000–1,500ft, and following acquisition of a target on the ASV screen, the typical Leigh Light procedure is as follows:

- The ASV operator informs the crew that he has a contact, and gives the pilot a course to steer.
- The navigator gives the aircraft's position to the wireless operator, who transmits a sighting report to base.
- The navigator goes back to lower the Leigh Light, then goes forward to the nose gun.
- The pilot turns on to the target heading, and begins a shallow dive (to lose height and gain speed) while the second pilot goes forward to control the light from the bomb aimer's position, straddled by the navigator manning the nose gun for flak suppression; bomb doors are opened.
- The ASV operator calls out ranges every half mile (and course corrections if necessary), then as the range falls below one mile (with

height approximately 250ft), the Leigh Light is switched on, the second pilot slewing it as required to illuminate and identify the target; drift can be judged and set on the azimuth dial, and the other dial is usually set to a 15° undershoot, then gently raised to find the target.

- As the aircraft passes over the target at around 50ft, the pilot releases the depth charges (with 60ft separation) and flame float markers.
- The rear gunner continues the flak suppression while watching for results of the attack, and the Leigh Light is switched off.

The pilot must continue to fly on instruments even after the light is switched on, as if he follows the light beam visually while it is being steered, he could easily become disoriented, which is dangerous at such a low level. ASV may be switched off after picking up a target in order to reduce the chances of detection by the U-boat's radar-warning receiver during the approach.

BELOW Leigh Light procedure: (1) Target detected by ASV radar; (2) When closer than one mile, the Leigh Light is switched on for final homing; (3) Depth charges released passing over target; (4) Light extinguished and aircraft climbs away to observe results. *(Author)*

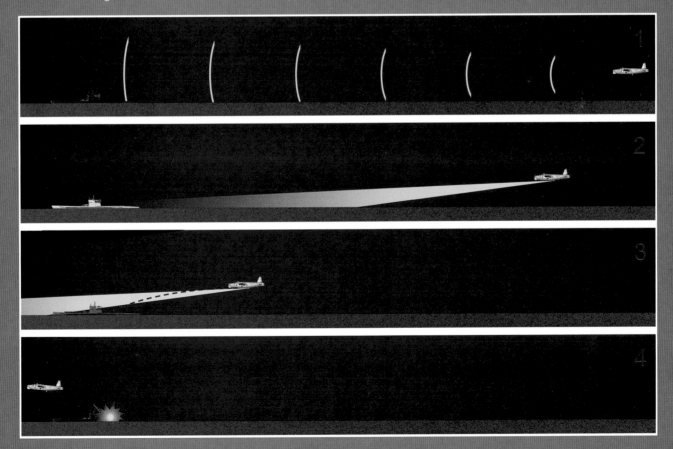

Command in January 1943 – this had a rotating scanner giving 360° coverage and used much shorter wavelengths than Mk II, so was far less susceptible to unwanted returns from the sea, making shipping targets easier to distinguish on the operator's screen, and these could be seen down to about 400yd range. Crucially, it was also undetectable by Metox, and it took the Germans some time to develop a detector for Mk III (Naxos).

Now aware of the capabilities of Leigh Light aircraft, the anti-aircraft armament on U-boats was improved – from a single 20mm gun to (typically) a 37mm gun plus two double 20mm guns – giving the submarine a chance of engaging the approaching aircraft to bring it down, or at least spoil its aim. This proved successful, with many aircraft being shot down or damaged during attacks. Eventually a single

Vickers K gun was fitted in the top part of the nose glazing to deter U-boat gunners, but often, rather than attack, aircraft would circle a surfaced U-boat at a safe distance until reinforcements arrived in the form of surface vessels or other aircraft. On later aircraft, pilot sighting was superseded by a Mk III low-level bombsight used by the Leigh Light operator.

The first U-boat to be sunk by a Leigh Light Wellington was in July 1942, and in their first year of operation, they sank another three U-boats and seriously damaged eight others – and also the morale of many other crews who encountered the aircraft. An additional benefit for Coastal Command was a rise in the number of daytime sightings, as more U-boats elected to stay submerged by night. However, U-boat sightings remained comparatively rare, and many crews who endured long patrols across great swathes of ocean could fly an entire tour without seeing one.

In total, five squadrons operated Leigh Light Wellingtons – a detachment of 172 at Skitten in northern Scotland became 179 Squadron in September 1942, moving to Gibraltar in November, then to Cornwall 18 months later. No 612 Squadron converted to the aircraft, starting in November 1942, being joined by 407 from January 1943 and by 304 from June. These squadrons sank 32 U-boats and damaged 20 more. Nos 304 and 612 Squadrons also used their Wellingtons for anti-E-boat patrols from East Anglia for a time (armed with 250lb bombs), and the aircraft was used as an anti-shipping 'pathfinder', locating enemy convoys with ASV and dropping flares to distract attention from incoming strike aircraft or MTBs. A total of 144 Coastal Command

Wellingtons were lost on operations, including 111 Leigh Light aircraft, with another 37 lost on non-operational flights (mostly Leigh Light training flights).

Service with Operational Training Units

At the start of the war, RAF squadrons were responsible for training their own crews, but this became unsustainable once operational flying was in progress. Operational Training Units were then formed to bring recruits up to combat readiness, before posting to squadrons. These units used a variety of training aircraft, but exposure to operational types was essential, and many OTUs were equipped partly or wholly with Wellingtons. OTU aircraft were typically fitted with dual flying controls (first tested in L4217 in 1938), with a duplicate control column and throttle controls for the second pilot. These were typically aircraft retired from operations (as were the instructors), so they were often not in peak condition and, combined with the inexperience of the crews, this led to high losses on the OTUs – up to the end of 1942, just over 900 Wellingtons crashed in the UK (from all causes) and 50% of these aircraft were serving with OTUs. This proportion rose steadily as front-line Wellington numbers declined and the use of the aircraft at OTUs increased, with a peak of 26 OTUs operating the aircraft by the end of 1943 (this compares with the peak of 25 operational squadrons two years earlier). OTUs typically had around 54 aircraft, three times the number of an operational squadron. OTU crews near the end of their training occasionally took part in operations, typically flying 'nickel' sorties.

The OTUs continued to operate the aircraft post-war with T.10 trainers, and it was these aircraft that saw the final RAF service by Wellingtons in 1953; most were on their last legs and were scrapped immediately.

Other UK service

Wellingtons served with Fighter Command's 527 Squadron for a year from April 1945, performing radar calibration duties. Small numbers also served with several Fleet Air Arm squadrons, mostly on training duties.

Service with other air forces

The Free French Air Force flew bombers as RAF 344 Squadron, which was re-mustered in November 1943 as *Flotille* (Squadron) 2F of the *Aéronavale* (French Fleet Air Arm), which operated the Wellington for maritime reconnaissance from Dakar in Senegal. The squadron moved to Port Lyautey (now Kenitra) in Morocco in 1950, and the Wellingtons were replaced by Lancasters in 1952. *Esquadrille* (flight) 10S was a test flight formed shortly after the end of the war, and operated three Wellingtons from Hyères and detachment bases in southern France for a few years. *Esquadrille* 51S was formed as a training flight in 1946 at Khouribga in Morocco, and operated Wellingtons to train navy pilots until 1950. In all, several dozen Wellingtons served under French command after the war.

THE WELLINGTON AT THE MOVIES

The Lion has Wings (1939) was a propaganda film produced by Alexander Korda, which begins with a 25-minute documentary section comparing life in Britain with life under Hitler, illustrated with newsreel footage that includes Wellingtons being built at Weybridge. The second section of the film shows the preparation and delivery of an RAF daylight attack on

the Kiel Canal, with a Wellington seen taking off and many shots of the crew at their stations as they fly to Germany and successfully bomb a warship, then fly back after repelling a fighter attack in which the Vickers turrets are seen in action. Acted scenes featuring Ralph Richardson and Merle Oberon attempted to link the segments of the film together, but these did little more than distract from the documentary elements of the film.

Target for Tonight (1941) was a more realistic (but still idealised) portrayal of an RAF bombing mission to Germany, which is notable for the fact that all of the 'actors' in the film are actually RAF men performing their real roles, including the AOC of Bomber Command Sir Richard Peirse. The film mostly follows the crew of Wellington R1296 'F for Freddie' as they fly to Germany, again successfully bombing their target and returning home. The pilot was played by Percy Pickard, who would later distinguish himself for real by commanding the RAF

(Jonathan Falconer collection)

element of Operation Biting, the raid on the German radar station at Bruneval in 1942. He also took part in Operation Jericho, which successfully bombed Amiens Prison in 1944 to release French prisoners, but he did not return from this operation.

One of Our Aircraft is Missing (1942) took its name from the line commonly heard at the end of radio broadcasts about RAF operations, and was a product of the partnership of Michael Powell and Emeric Pressburger, with a cast headlined by Hugh Burden, Eric Portman and Googie Withers. Opening with the dramatic crash of an unmanned Wellington, it follows the aircraft's crew who had bailed out after it received flak damage. They land in occupied Holland, and most of the film tells the story of the Dutchmen who help them. Eventually they manage to escape in a rowing boat to a 'lobster pot'

rescue buoy, from where they radio for help. Peter Ustinov made his debut as a Dutch priest in the film, which was edited by David Lean. Again, there is footage of the Wellington taking off, and many shots of the crew undertaking their flying duties, including the bomb aimer at his CSBS, as well as the crew baling out through the entry hatch, the starboard rear emergency hatch, and the rear gunner from his turret.

The Dam Busters (1955) featured the Wellington in archive footage of BJ895 dropping the test 'bouncing bombs' at Chesil Beach (the bomb itself was matted out as the weapon was still secret at the time). The shot of the aircraft taking off was new footage of MF628, the aircraft travelling directly towards the camera to hide the fact that it was painted in the post-war all-silver trainer colour scheme. MF628 was also used as a camera platform for some of the air-to-air photography. In the film, when Wallis (Michael Redgrave) is trying to persuade the man from the Ministry to let him use a Wellington for his tests, he says: 'If you told them that I designed it, do you think that might help?', which rather overlooks Pierson's contribution!

Three South African Air Force squadrons operated Wellingtons. No 17 Squadron SAAF undertook anti-submarine and anti-shipping operations in the Mediterranean from autumn 1942 with Blenheims and Venturas, and in early 1945 were training in Egypt with Wellington Mk XIIIs in preparation for conversion to Warwicks, but the end of the war arrived before the new aircraft. No 26 Squadron SAAF was also formed in autumn 1942, initially as a bomber squadron, and became operational in May 1943 at Takoradi in the Gold Coast (now Ghana) with 16 Wellingtons, increasing to 26 (a mix of Mk Xs, XIs, XIIs, and XIIIs) for convoy escort and maritime reconnaissance duties. Eleven aircraft were dispatched to Dakar during April 1944 to assist with anti-submarine patrols there. A total of 13 squadron aircraft were lost on operations, mostly through accidents. Shortly after the end of the war, the aircraft were struck off and the squadron disbanded, personnel returning to South Africa. No 28 Squadron SAAF was formed as a transport squadron in the Mediterranean theatre in June 1943, and flew a range of aircraft including Wellingtons, but these were replaced at the end of the year.

Wellingtons flew in Greece with 38 Squadron and 221 Squadron on transport, bombing, and maritime patrol duties, and when the Royal Hellenic Air Force was formed at the end of the war, some aircraft passed to them. Around 20 Wellingtons (including ASV-equipped Mk XIIIs) flew with 13 Squadron RHAF based at Hassani, near Athens, but the aircraft were well worn when they were acquired, and were replaced by C-47s in 1947. No 355 Squadron RHAF also flew Wellingtons on transport duties.

A small number of Wellingtons that force-landed on the Continent were test flown by the Luftwaffe, including Mk IA L7788 of 311 (Czech) Squadron and Mk ICs T2501 of 99 Squadron and L7842 of 311 Squadron (one of whose crew was shot for his part in the 'Great Escape'). The Portuguese may have flown an interned Wellington Mk X that landed near Cape St Vincent in April 1943 during a transfer flight.

The last flight by a Wellington is believed to have been by T.10 MF628 from Aston Down

to Wisley in January 1955. This aircraft is now preserved by the RAF Museum.

(See Appendix 3 for details of the number of squadrons operating Wellingtons throughout the war.)

ABOVE Wellington Xs of 300 (Mazowiecki) Squadron at RAF Hemswell in June 1943. *(IWM CH10456)*

Summary

*T*he *Bomber Command War Diaries* record 47,409 Wellington sorties, dropping 42,000 tons of bombs and incurring losses of 1,727 aircraft. Operations flown from the UK total approximately 350,000 hours, with those from the Middle and Far East totalling 525,000 hours. Wartime training was probably over a million hours, with post-war training adding a further 350,000 hours.

By the time the last Wellington navigational trainer was retired from RAF service in 1953, the type had been in continuous use by the service for 15 years, a remarkable longevity in the light of the speed of aircraft development over this time. The aircraft served with every RAF Command as well as the Fleet Air Arm, and saw combat action across much of the world.

Chapter Three

Anatomy of the Wellington

The Wellington was a two-engined monoplane bomber of conventional outward appearance, but owed its unique reputation to its geodetic construction. The structure of the 'basketweave bomber' was only one aspect of its design, which allowed it to make a significant contribution to the war.

OPPOSITE Around 1994, the main sections of 'R for Robert' are complete and laid out ready for final assembly. *(Brooklands Museum)*

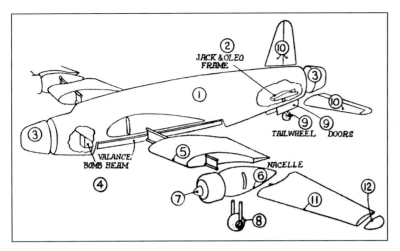

Introduction

The Wellington is a two-engined cantilever mid-wing medium bomber, fabricated from duralumin light alloy, the main structure is built using the Vickers-Wallis geodetic system and covered in doped fabric.

Air Publication 1578 describes the Wellington. This AP has many volumes and many versions, to describe operation, maintenance, and repair of all main marks of the aircraft. Construction and the equipment fitted varied between marks, types, and sometimes individual aircraft, with specific details varying considerably, so the descriptions below should be read as indicative only.

Fuselage

The fuselage is a geodetic tube incorporating four tubular longerons. The tube is made up from 20 separate panels, which are joined to make four main panels (top, bottom, and two sides); the top and bottom being nearly semi-circular in section and the sides slightly curved, giving a deep section overall. Each panel section is manufactured by subcontractors, and these sections are bolted or riveted to the longerons and to each other in construction jigs in the main factory, allowing the fuselage to be assembled in a few hours. Generally, each geodetic member begins at one longeron and winds spirally round the fuselage to end at the next longeron, special end gussets being used to attach them. All geodetics are sprayed with a primer and aluminium paint to resist corrosion.

To distribute the main structural forces, the fuselage is fitted with a series of annular internal frames at points of greatest stress, to which the wings, tail surfaces, bomb beam, and other structures are attached directly. These are at the 5½, 12½, 22½, 50½, 85 and 90 station positions (see page 25). Terminal rings are attached to the ends of the geodetic tube, and the turret mountings are cantilevered to these rings at the lower longeron position. Additional

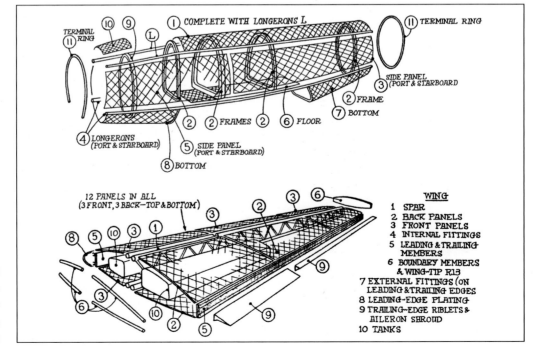

terminal frames are used to strengthen openings, such as the cockpit and bomb bay ends.

Side windows (where fitted) are made from a flexible transparent plastic, held in place by metal strips around the edges, bolted to the geodetics by 2BA bolts in oversized holes with rubber washers.

Crew entry is by the main hatch, which forms the floor of the bomb aimer's compartment. A short ladder is used to enter, this usually being taken into the aircraft and stowed in the fuselage. A corridor on the starboard side of the radio operator and navigator stations connects the cockpit to the mid-fuselage. The bomb bay roof forms the floor of the mid-fuselage, and is made from a flat panel of straight geodetic members, with plywood sheets laid on top.

Wings

Each wing consists of two main sections separated by, but connected through, the engine nacelle. The wing geodetics are terminated by tubular boundary members, one at each end of the inner wing, and one inboard on the outer wing. The wings use aerofoil section NACA 24 with an aspect ratio of 8.8:1 (compared to approximately 6.9:1 for

the Hampden and 6.2:1 for the Whitley), and are mounted 4° nose-up relative to the aircraft datum. Aerodynamic interference between the wing and fuselage is minimised by the mid-wing position and fillets applied around the junctions.

The main spar is made up of four alloy tubes (one pair at the top and one pair at the bottom) connected by zig-zag spacing members to form a Warren truss. The portion outboard of station 26 on the outer wing has only one tube top and one bottom, these being joined to the end of the double tube by serrated steel plates top and bottom, which are bolted through the ends of the tubes. The main spar is not connected to the fuselage structure directly, but passes through reinforced holes at station 40; the

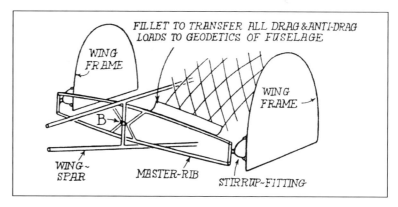

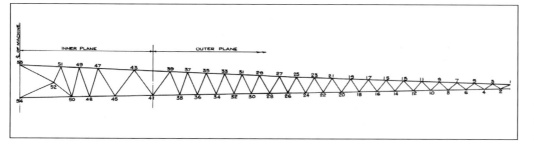

RIGHT Section of wing spar tube from L4288 (actual size). *(Author)*

BELOW Looking forwards from the trailing edge frame of N2980, showing the main spar with centreline spar box. The handwheels just aft of it are the fuel cocks. The frame of the floor can be seen, but normally this would have been covered by plywood sheeting. *(Author)*

BELOW RIGHT The bottom of the main spar, where the inboard double tube connects to the outboard single tube. Note the gusset plate connecting them and the grooved interface between. *(Author)*

RIGHT The fuselage side of the Brooklands walk-through exhibit, showing the opening for the main spar. *(Author)*

FAR RIGHT N2980's main spar passing through the starboard fuselage side. *(Author)*

double-tube spars are pin jointed on the aircraft centreline. The main spar and longerons are made from high-tensile duralumin.

Secondary spars fore and aft, each consisting of two alloy C-tubes (one top and one bottom) separated by a flat 20SWG plate, are located just aft of the leading edge and just ahead of the trailing edge. They complete the structure of the flattened geodetic tube that forms each wing and carry the wing shear loads to the fuselage via Cardan joints bolted to the leading edge (22½) and trailing edge (50½) frames around the fuselage geodetics. The leading edge is a curved duralumin plate with internal stiffeners bolted to the 18SWG tubes of the leading edge spar with a fabric covering and (in later aircraft) a $1/16$in mild steel plate on top riveted to the stiffeners as protection from balloon cables. The trailing edge spar carries the flaps (inboard) and ailerons (outboard); tubes are 16SWG. Duralumin wingtip fittings bolted to the ends of the spars carry the navigation and formation-keeping lights behind Perspex covers.

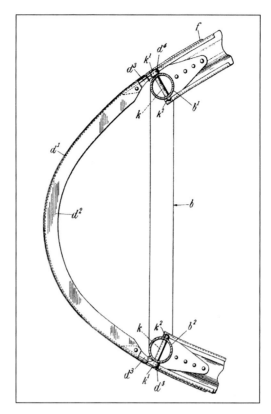

LEFT Detail of the wing leading edge construction and attachment to the geodetic panels. *(BAE Systems)*

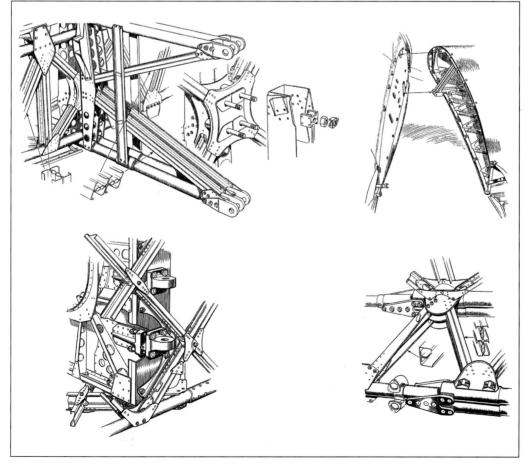

LEFT Main spar details (clockwise from top left): the main spar root, attaching the outer wing to the nacelle; main spar where the double tube meets the single tube; the attachments on the fuselage frames for attaching the wings. *(Courtesy of Flight International)*

The surface structure of each wing is made from geodetic panels, one top and one bottom for the inner wing section and six top and six bottom for the outer wing section (these being divided up for manufacturing convenience).

Wing fabric is bolted to the geodetics at the leading and trailing edges and sewn to angle fittings using waxed string. The leading edge is then bolted to the front spar and the joint taped over. Some aircraft have Martin-Baker balloon cable cutters on the leading edges.

The heated pitot head for the airspeed

ABOVE Detail of the wing leading edge and spar with the internal fuel tanks on their wooden runners. *(Author)*

BELOW The starboard wing. *(Author)*

BELOW RIGHT The pitot head beneath the starboard wing. *(Author)*

indicator is mounted beneath the starboard outer wing, 2ft 2in below the wing underside.

Empennage

The three empennage surfaces are of cantilevered geodetic construction covered by fabric (except the outboard third which has a duralumin stressed skin), and have a two-tube main spar and built-up leading and trailing edge spars. These are attached to the main fuselage frames at stations 85 and 90 and also to partial frames at stations 81 (fin) and 82 (horizontal stabilisers). Control surfaces are also fabric-covered, their main structural member being an alloy tube which pivots in roller bearings on horseshoe-shaped steel brackets attached to the back of the rear spar; rotation of these tubes moves the surfaces, and is effected by short throw arms connected by push-pull rods to the pilot's flight controls. Elevators are horn balanced (mass balanced on prototypes) and the rudder is mass balanced; all three control surfaces have trim tabs operated by cable from the cockpit, elevator trim being interlinked with the flap controls. The rudder incorporates the tail navigation lights in its trailing edge. Mk II and later aircraft have enlarged horizontal stabilisers, with 12in longer chord at the root; later Mk Xs have a modified horn balance shape.

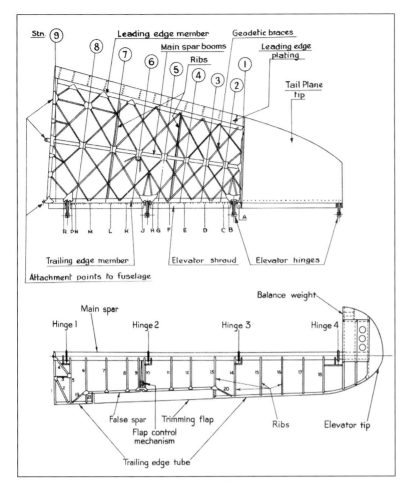

Stn. ⑨

Leading edge member
Main spar booms
Ribs
⑧ ⑦ ⑥ ⑤ ④ ③ ② ①
Geodetic braces
Leading edge plating
Tail Plane tip

R P N M L K J H G F E D C B A

Trailing edge member
Attachment points to fuselage
Elevator shroud
Elevator hinges

Balance weight
Main spar
Hinge 1   Hinge 2   Hinge 3   Hinge 4
4 6 7 8 9 10 11 12 13 14 15 16 17 18
3 5
19 21
20

False spar   Trimming flap
Flap control mechanism
Trailing edge tube
Ribs
Elevator tip

ABOVE The horizontal stabiliser and elevator. This is a broad-chord tailplane introduced with the Mk II. *(Crown Copyright via The National Archives)*

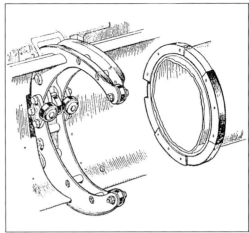

ABOVE Detail of the steel horseshoe brackets with roller bearings, which carry the elevator tube. *(Courtesy of* Flight International*)*

ABOVE The starboard horizontal stabiliser. Clearly seen are the three ribs connecting to the fuselage frames, as well as the tube mounting of the elevator. *(Author)*

FIN TIP
RIB
GEODETIC BRACES
MAIN SPAR BOOMS
RIB
① ② ③ ④ ⑤
G H J K L M N P Q
STN ⑥
LEADING EDGE PLATING
LEADING EDGE MEMBER
ATTACHMENT POINTS TO FUSELAGE
RUDDER HINGES
RUDDER SHROUD
A B C D E F
TRAILING EDGE MEMBER

MASS BALANCE
TRAILING EDGE TUBE
RIBS
HINGE 4
2 3 4 5 6 7 8 9 10 11 12 13 14 15 16 17 18 19
HINGE 3
HINGE 2
HINGE 1
MAIN SPAR
FALSE SPAR
COMBINED TRIMMING AND BALANCER FLAP

LEFT The fin and rudder. *(Crown Copyright via The National Archives)*

Cutaway of Wellington Mk XIV, MP714, the only example known to have been fitted with rocket projectiles. *(Mike Badrocke)*

1 Nash and Thompson power-operated tail gun turret
2 Four Browning 0.303in (7.7mm) machine guns
3 Cartridge case ejection chute
4 Elevator tab
5 Elevator rib construction
6 Elevator horn balance
7 Tailplane tip construction
8 R.3003 aerial cable
9 Tailplane leading-edge de-icing boot
10 Tailplane geodetic construction
11 Elevator torque shaft
12 Fin/tailplane attachment main frames
13 Gun turret entry doors
14 Rudder tab
15 Tail navigation and formation lights
16 Rudder rib construction
17 Rudder mass-balance weights
18 HF aerial cable
19 Fin tip construction
20 Tailfin geodetic construction
21 Leading-edge de-icing boot
22 Starboard fabric-covered elevator
23 Aluminium alloy-skinned tailplane tip segment
24 Port fabric-covered tailplane
25 Tailplane control rods
26 Ammunition feed chutes
27 Tail wheel pivot fixing
28 Castoring tail wheel
29 Ventral aerial mast
30 Tail wheel retraction jack
31 Vacuum flask stowage
32 Tail turret ammunition boxes
33 Boarding ladder stowage
34 Life jacket container
35 Engine turning crank handle
36 Radio altimeter aerial
37 Fuselage fabric covering
38 Lower longeron
39 Footboards
40 Browning 0.303in (7.7mm) machine gun
41 Beam gunner's window, port and starboard
42 Ammunition box
43 Beam gunner's swivelling seat
44 Reconnaissance flares
45 Leigh Light mounting frames
46 Hydraulic actuator
47 Light extension and retraction mechanism
48 Leigh Light control panel
49 Fuselage upper longeron
50 Cabin roof geodetic frame construction
51 Beam approach aerial
52 Fabric support stringers
53 Mid-cabin window panels, port and starboard
54 Flare/marker launch tube
55 Rear spar attachment main frame
56 Marine marker stowage
57 Toilet
58 TR.9J transmitter/receiver
59 Dinghy emergency equipment pack
60 ASV radar operator's seat
61 Intercom socket
62 Parachute stowage
63 Astrodome observation hatch
64 ASV Mk III radar receiver
65 Radar equipment rack
66 Wing main spar cut-out
67 Pneumatic system CO_2 bottles

68 Oil filler cap
69 Starboard engine oil tank, 16 Imp gal (73 l) capacity
70 Nacelle fuel tank, 58 Imp gal (264 l) capacity
71 Main undercarriage hydraulic retraction jack
72 Dinghy inflation bottle
73 Dinghy stowage
74 Leigh Light, extended
75 Searchlight cooling air scoop
76 Rear spar
77 Flap shroud ribs
78 Fuel jettison pipe
79 Starboard split trailing-edge flap

80 Aileron trim tab
81 Starboard aileron
82 Aileron rib construction
83 Starboard formation light
84 Wing-tip fairing
85 Starboard navigation light
86 Armoured leading-edge panel
87 Geodetic wing panel construction
88 Outer wing panel spar joint
89 Pitot head
90 60lb (27kg) air-to-surface rocket projectile
91 Leading-edge nose ribs
92 Main spar
93 Starboard wing fuel tank bays; total fuel capacity, 750 Imp gal (3,410 l)
94 Front spar
95 Rocket launch rails
96 Main wheel doors
97 Starboard main wheel
98 Hydraulic brake pipe
99 Oleo-pneumatic shock absorber leg strut

100 Main undercarriage pivot fixing
101 Engine bay fireproof bulkhead
102 Engine bearer struts
103 Oil cooler exhaust duct
104 Adjustable engine bay cooling air gills
105 Oil cooler
106 Oil cooler air scoop
107 Three-segment detachable engine cowling panels
108 Flame suppressing exhaust pipe on inboard side
109 Engine mounting ring frame
110 Carburettor air intake duct

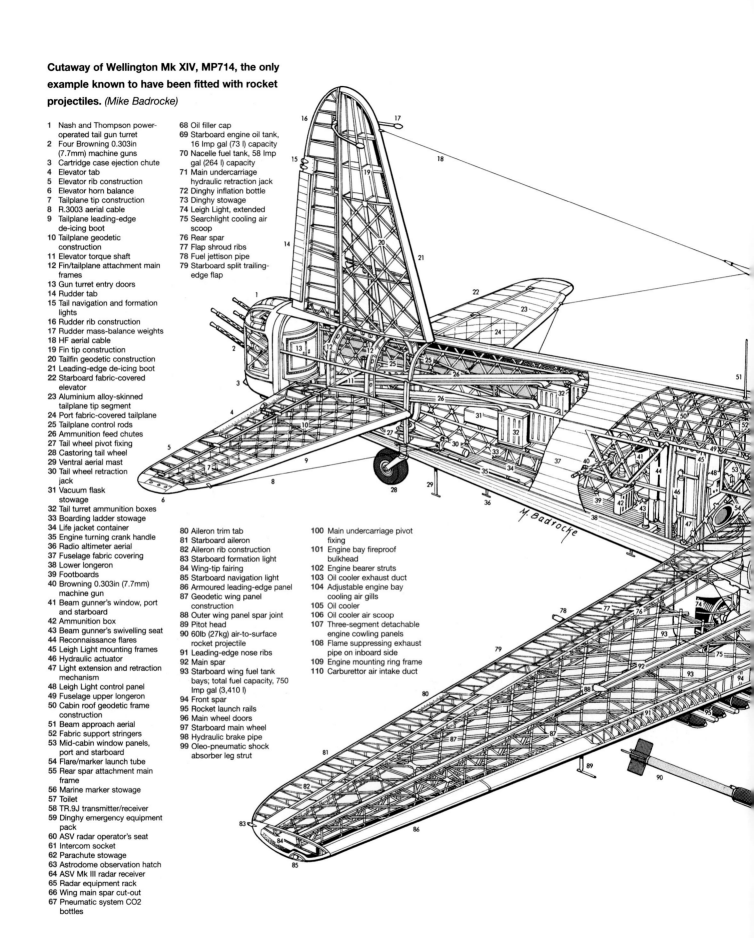

M. Badrocke

64

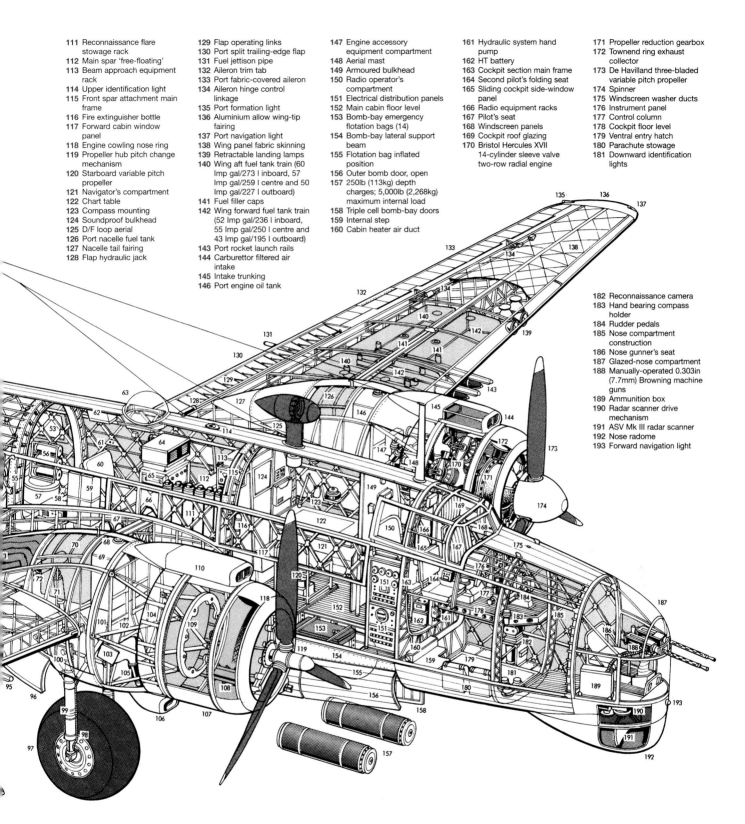

111 Reconnaissance flare stowage rack
112 Main spar 'free-floating'
113 Beam approach equipment rack
114 Upper identification light
115 Front spar attachment main frame
116 Fire extinguisher bottle
117 Forward cabin window panel
118 Engine cowling nose ring
119 Propeller hub pitch change mechanism
120 Starboard variable pitch propeller
121 Navigator's compartment
122 Chart table
123 Compass mounting
124 Soundproof bulkhead
125 D/F loop aerial
126 Port nacelle fuel tank
127 Nacelle tail fairing
128 Flap hydraulic jack

129 Flap operating links
130 Port split trailing-edge flap
131 Fuel jettison pipe
132 Aileron trim tab
133 Port fabric-covered aileron
134 Aileron hinge control linkage
135 Port formation light
136 Aluminium allow wing-tip fairing
137 Port navigation light
138 Wing panel fabric skinning
139 Retractable landing lamps
140 Wing aft fuel tank train (60 Imp gal/273 l inboard, 57 Imp gal/259 l centre and 50 Imp gal/227 l outboard)
141 Fuel filler caps
142 Wing forward fuel tank train (52 Imp gal/236 l inboard, 55 Imp gal/250 l centre and 43 Imp gal/195 l outboard)
143 Port rocket launch rails
144 Carburettor filtered air intake
145 Intake trunking
146 Port engine oil tank

147 Engine accessory equipment compartment
148 Aerial mast
149 Armoured bulkhead
150 Radio operator's compartment
151 Electrical distribution panels
152 Main cabin floor level
153 Bomb-bay emergency flotation bags (14)
154 Bomb-bay lateral support beam
155 Flotation bag inflated position
156 Outer bomb door, open
157 250lb (113kg) depth charges; 5,000lb (2,268kg) maximum internal load
158 Triple cell bomb-bay doors
159 Internal step
160 Cabin heater air duct

161 Hydraulic system hand pump
162 HT battery
163 Cockpit section main frame
164 Second pilot's folding seat
165 Sliding cockpit side-window panel
166 Radio equipment racks
167 Pilot's seat
168 Windscreen panels
169 Cockpit roof glazing
170 Bristol Hercules XVII 14-cylinder sleeve valve two-row radial engine

171 Propeller reduction gearbox
172 Townend ring exhaust collector
173 De Havilland three-bladed variable pitch propeller
174 Spinner
175 Windscreen washer ducts
176 Instrument panel
177 Control column
178 Cockpit floor level
179 Ventral entry hatch
180 Parachute stowage
181 Downward identification lights

182 Reconnaissance camera
183 Hand bearing compass holder
184 Rudder pedals
185 Nose compartment construction
186 Nose gunner's seat
187 Glazed-nose compartment
188 Manually-operated 0.303in (7.7mm) Browning machine guns
189 Ammunition box
190 Radar scanner drive mechanism
191 ASV Mk III radar scanner
192 Nose radome
193 Forward navigation light

Fabric covering

Because of the flexibility of the geodetic framework, metal skin cannot be used, and the airframe is covered in Irish linen (Madapolam where possible), which is painted with several layers of dope to seal and tighten the fabric.

A series of wooden rails are bolted to the fuselage geodetics in a fore-and-aft direction, and the fabric is laid over these (giving the fuselage its distinctive ribbed appearance). Some 'locking' rails have a flattened groove in the outer surface, allowing a thin wooden capping strip to be placed over the fabric and pressed into the groove, where it is screwed to the rail beneath to hold the fabric in place.

The linen is in strips approximately 6ft wide, being applied to the fuselage diagonally to allow the cloth bias to stretch over the curved surface (the diagonal application also prevents long tears developing in the covering, but this is of secondary importance). The cloth strips are sewn together, with double balloon seams at eight stitches to the inch.

The fabric attachment on the wings is somewhat different. A method of attachment using interlocking pins was patented (GB504565) but was dropped in favour of a simpler method using piano wire skewers and headless 6BA bolts. The bolts have holes drilled through them at one end to suit the skewers, and several are threaded on to a length of wire, then the long ends of the bolts are passed through the fabric and through holes drilled in the geodetics, and finally a nut is screwed on inside to pull the skewer (and the fabric trapped beneath it) down on to the geodetic member. As the skewers run along the geodetic members, this gives the wings a quilted appearance, especially in flight. This method is used for the panels ahead of the main spar; aft of the spar and on the tail surfaces, string is used to hold the skewers instead of bolts. Unlike the fuselage, the geodetic panels making up each wing are covered before the panels are attached. As the fuselage covering involves sewing, this is usually done by female workers, but as the wing covering is bolted on, this is usually done by male workers! About 8,000 screws are used to attach the covering.

The fabric seams, fuselage locking strips, and piano wires on the wings are all covered by strips of tape to make them smooth, and the covering is given several layers of dope to weatherproof it. Early aircraft have four coats of red oxide dope plus one coat of coloured dope; on later aircraft, the standard coating is as follows:

- One (sometimes two) brushed coats of red oxide dope, to seal the fabric (this gives the covering its red colouring when seen from inside).
- Up to seven brushed coats of clear dope, to tighten the fabric as required.
- One (sometimes two) sprayed coats of aluminium dope, for UV protection.
- One coat of white dope, to act as an undercoat for the camouflage layer (sometimes omitted).
- One (sometimes two) sprayed coats of coloured dope, to give the required colour scheme.

The dope layers together weigh approximately 7½oz/sq yd. Metal parts are given one coat of primer (sometimes over a coat of clear dope) beneath the camouflage layer.

Flaps

Trailing edge three-section Schrenk flaps are alloy-skinned on the lower surface and are operated by double-acting hydraulic jacks mounted in the trailing edge ribs of the inner wing, tubular push rods connecting these to the flap ribs. In the raised position, the rods lie at an angle to the operating shafts, so that inboard movement of the shaft causes the flaps to be thrust downwards.

Although the flaps on each wing are operated by their own hydraulic jack, they are interconnected to ensure that the flap settings on both sides are approximately equal (by a hydraulic link on early aircraft and a mechanical scissor link from the IC onwards). The flaps are protected by a shroud fitted above them, which is supported by a row of forged aluminium

LEFT Method of fabric attachment on the fuselage. Grooved wooden strips are screwed to geodetics, then capping strips are screwed in to hold fabric in place; a cover strip is added before the covering is doped. *(Author)*

LEFT Method of fabric attachment on the wings. Loops of string around piano wires hold the fabric against the geodetics. As with the fuselage a cover strip is added before the covering is doped. *(Author)*

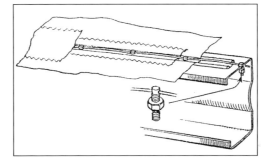

LEFT Detail of fabric attachment on the wings, showing the piano wire threaded on to headless bolts. *(Courtesy of* Flight International*)*

RIGHT The metal-skinned Schrenk flaps on the starboard wing. *(Author)*

brackets and extends the wing top surface to the trailing edge. As the shroud is fixed and the act of lowering the flaps opens them away from it, they are also known as split flaps.

The aircraft becomes slightly tail-heavy when the flaps are lowered, so the elevator trimming tabs and flaps are interconnected via a system of pulleys in the trimming tab control cables, in order to automatically maintain longitudinal trim as the flaps are lowered. The pilot must ensure that the aircraft is not already trimmed nose-down when lowering the flaps, otherwise the automatic trim mechanism will be damaged. The flap control does not have any preset positions, consisting only of a selector for 'up' or 'down' and a gauge indicating flap position; flaps can be lowered to a maximum of 70°.

Ailerons

Outboard of the flaps, Frise ailerons are attached to the trailing edge spar by five hinges. Each aileron has a full-length main spar with nose and trailing edge ribs, the nose ribs being covered in a duralumin plate, which also covers the mass balance. The port aileron has a small trim tab fitted near its inboard end, which can be adjusted in flight; the starboard side tab can only be adjusted on the ground.

Nacelles

The main function of the nacelles is to connect the engines to the airframe, but they also house the main undercarriage legs and their retraction gear, reserve fuel tanks, oil tanks, and fire extinguisher bottles. The starboard nacelle contains a dinghy beneath a panel on the top surface.

The nacelles are manufactured in two halves, and are of monocoque stressed-skin construction in 16SWG duralumin. The main and secondary spars pass through and support the nacelles, which are attached by bolts passing through special fittings connecting the top and bottom of the main spar. Spring-loaded bolts (14 inboard and 12 outboard) pass through the tubular boundary members at the ends of the wing sections, to engage with threaded butterfly fittings riveted to the outside of the nacelle. In this way, the nacelle forms a continuation of the structure of the wing.

The front of the nacelle is a flat fireproof bulkhead, consisting of 1/8in asbestos between two 22SWG duralumin sheets.

Bomb bay

The bomb bay is a single compartment over 23ft long beneath the bottom longerons, running from station 12 to station 56. Usually it is fitted with a bomb beam consisting of two vertical trusses connected by inverted U-shaped arches and slung between the 12½ frame and the leading and trailing edge frames, the weight of the bomb load thus being transmitted directly to the wing spars. The beam divides the bomb bay lengthways into three cells, the trusses incorporating bomb slips to which bombs of up to 500lb are attached. Additional beams to carry 1,000lb, 2,000lb and

4,000lb bombs, torpedoes or mines can be fitted, either between the trusses or in place of the standard beam (see below). Maximum bomb load is 4,500lb, this being reduced if overload fuel tanks are being carried.

The bomb bay opening is covered by five sets of doors – two curved sets outboard on the outer cells attached to fixed valances extending below the lower longerons, two flat sets attached to the bomb beams inboard on the outer cells, plus one set covering the centre cell hinged on the port sides of the bomb beam. Each set consists of six separate doors formed from a duralumin frame covered in fabric on Mk I and IA and fibreboard on later marks. The hinges are developed from those on the Wellesley and patented in 1938 (GB479858), which use internal springs to open the doors and hydraulic pressure to close them, except for the forward door in each set which is both opened and closed hydraulically; each door is connected at its outer edge to its neighbours by a sliding $3/16$in bar, to keep each set of doors

BELOW Two parallel trusses formed the bomb beam, which was hung from the three fuselage frames. *(Crown Copyright via The National Archives)*

ABOVE Inboard face of the starboard nacelle from inside the wing ahead of the main spar (left) and behind (right). The air cylinders are for the 200psi pneumatic system. *(Author)*

BELOW Detail of the attachment of the front of the bomb beam to the 12½ frame. *(Author)*

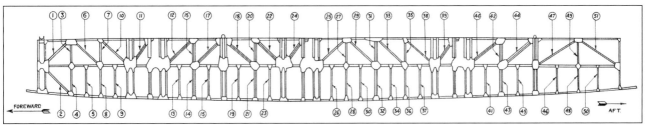

ABOVE The three compartments of the standard bomb bay. Note the crutching arms and the perforated plates that held the flotation bags. *(Author)*

RIGHT Section through the bomb bay, showing door openings and bomb beam with two-tier bomb crutches. *(Crown Copyright)*

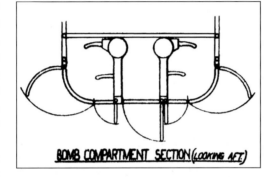

BOMB COMPARTMENT SECTION *(LOOKING AFT.)*

in line. A length of rubber tubing is attached to the outer edge of each door to act as a seal when the door is closed; in the outer cell, the curved outer doors close first, followed by the inner doors. The fifth door of the outboard cells is detachable to allow smoke to be discharged from tanks carried in these cells.

All doors are opened and closed simultaneously by rotation of a handle on the left side of the pilot's instrument panel; the handle is interlinked with the master switch, preventing bombs from being released while the doors are closed.

The Type D.III electro-magnetic bomb release is a self-contained unit consisting of a screened coil in a Bakelite housing with shoulders at each end carrying the armature trip levers. A 'bomb gone' switch is broken by the opening of the bomb hook, and the indicator light going out thus means that the jaws are open.

Two windows in the rear of the bomb bay can be used to check visually that all bombs have been released.

Undercarriage

The undercarriage is of Vickers construction, with oleo-pneumatic shock absorber struts containing oil and compressed air; air pressure can be altered (on the ground) for different all-up weights. Vickers pneumatic brakes and

RIGHT The bomb bay rear bulkhead, showing the two windows for visual inspection of the bomb bay. *(Author)*

FAR RIGHT Detail of the bomb bay hinges and valance. *(Author)*

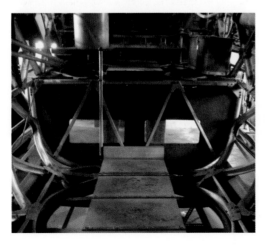

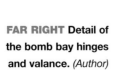

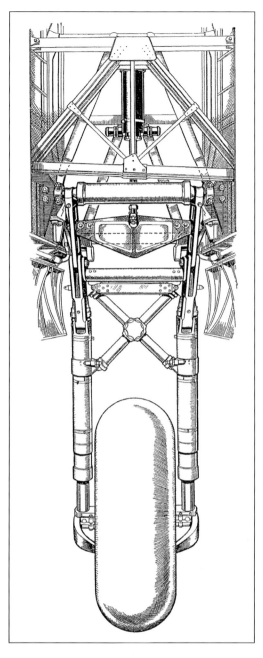

spring-loaded lock-down pins are fitted, and the undercarriage is raised hydraulically by a single jack on each gear, which pulls on a transverse yolk folding the backstay and rotating the main struts backwards into the underside of the nacelle, four-part 22SWG duralumin-skinned doors closing around the wheel automatically. Mk I aircraft have Dunlop AH.2197 wheels and Dunlop tyres that retract completely; Mk IA and later aircraft have larger Dunlop AH.10158 wheels that remain partly protruding from the nacelle, rubber strips on the edges of the nacelle doors sealing against the tyre. Each main wheel weighs 300lb.

The castoring tail wheel (Dunlop AH.2186 on Mk II and earlier aircraft, AH.10223 otherwise) retracts hydraulically into the tail frame assembly, which also carries bolts for the attachment of tail ballast. Mk I and IA aircraft have two doors linked to the tail wheel support, which thus open and close automatically with the wheel; later marks have no doors. Early tail wheel forks were rounded one-part steel forgings, while later forks were welded together. If the throttles are closed while the undercarriage is retracted, a horn behind the pilot will sound.

ABOVE Detail of the starboard main undercarriage. Note the hydraulic hinges for closing the gear doors. *(Author)*

BELOW The port main undercarriage from the rear. Note the cut-outs in the doors that fit around the partially exposed wheel. *(Author)*

ABOVE The starboard main undercarriage from astern, with the main spar passing through the nacelle (top), the retraction jack (behind) that folds the backstay, pulling the main oleo frame (bottom) with the wheel up behind it; the red tube is a ground lock. *(Author)*

BELOW The starboard main undercarriage, showing the oleos. The gear is resting on axle stands to preserve the tyres. *(Author)*

Pilot's controls

The pilot's control column is topped by a spectacles-type handwheel. Trim controls for elevators and ailerons are mounted to the left of his seat, ahead of which the throttles and other main engine/propeller controls are grouped together in a box.

Most marks of aircraft are fitted with a pneumatically powered automatic pilot (a Mk IV on aircraft prior to Mk X and a Mk VIII on later aircraft) mounted beneath the cockpit floor, with a gyroscope providing aileron and elevator servo motor control; rudder control is provided on the Mk VIII system only. The automatic pilot does not compensate for changes in trim as the aircraft lightens.

The control surfaces are operated by a system of push-pull rods running in roller bearings along the port side of the fuselage, the aileron rods branching off into the wings at the trailing edge frame. Rod sections are connected by screwed spindles and sleeves and supported in guide brackets. Trimming tabs on the elevators, rudder, and port aileron are operated by cables following similar paths through the aircraft.

The control column, rudder bar, trimming tab control units, and autopilot units are assembled on the flying control platform in the cockpit, which is bolted to the bulkhead and front frames. The control column is a hollow shaft with an internal torque tube with the aileron lever at its base, which is linked to a horizontal countershaft attached to the control rods and a geared sector engaging the autopilot. The torque tube is rotated by the pilot's handwheel through a small bevel wheel and quadrant; handwheel rotation is limited by two screws with lock nuts. The handwheel also carries two handles that operate the main wheel brakes; the handles pull a Bowden cable that runs down the centre of the column to a pneumatic valve unit under the floor, which activates the brakes. The handles can be locked in position for parking and should be used gently to avoid tipping the aircraft on to its nose. Torpedoes (if carried) are released by push-buttons attached to the handwheel.

The control column is riveted to a cross-

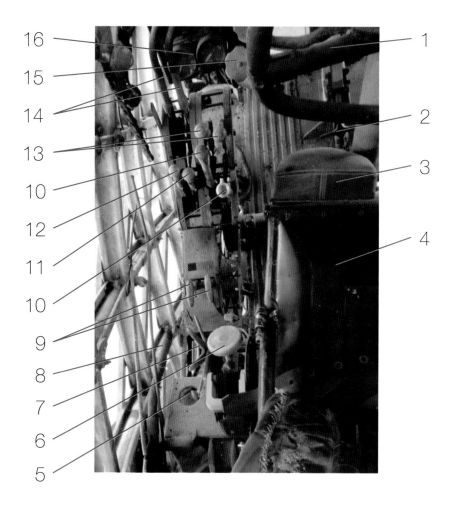

ABOVE The pilot's controls to the left of his seat. *(Author)*

1 Pilot's handwheel
2 Reach adjustment for rudder bar (star wheel)
3 Knee cushion
4 Pilot's seat
5 Port aileron trim tab control (missing)
6 Elevator and rudder trim tab control
7 Elevator trim tab fine control (star wheel)
8 Landing lights retraction lever
9 Slow-running engine cut-outs port and starboard (P&S)
10 Airscrew pitch control levers P&S
11 Hot/cold air intake control lever
12 Two-speed supercharger control lever
13 Mixture control levers P&S
14 Throttle control levers P&S
15 Compressed air supply for fuel jettison system
16 Oxygen regulator system

shaft carrying a lever to the elevator control rods and another geared sector engaging the autopilot. The rudder bar is mounted on a slide connected to a short vertical shaft carrying a lever to the rudder control rods and another geared sector engaging the autopilot (if fitted). The rudder bar can be adjusted for leg reach by means of a star wheel and screw spindle in

ABOVE The main instrument panel. *(Author)*

1 Oil pressure gauge (starboard engine)
2 Oil temperature gauge (starboard engine)
3 Clock
4 Flap control lever
5 Compass
6 Undercarriage control lever
7 Safety catch for undercarriage control lever
8 Oil temperature gauge (port engine)
9 Engine boost gauges reversal switch
10 Pilot's rudder bar
11 Pilot's rudder trim control
12 Oil pressure gauge (port engine)
13 Cowling gills control handle (starboard engine)
14 Pilot's control column
15 Signalling switchbox for identification lamps
16 Signalling switchbox for formation-keeping lamps
17 Compressed air control for fuel jettison system

18 Oxygen regulator unit
19 Hot/Cold air intake control lever
20 Two-speed supercharger control lever
21 Airscrew pitch control lever
22 Mixture control levers P&S
23 Throttle control levers P&S
24 Pilot's control yoke
25 Wheel brake levers (not connected)
26 Bomb doors control handle
27 Instrument flying panel:
   top row: airspeed indicator, artificial horizon, vertical speed indicator
   bottom row: altimeter, heading indicator, turn and slip indicator
28 Auto controls 'nose/tail heavy' and main pressure gauge
29 Beam approach system visual indicator
30 Starter push switch (port engine)
31 Boost pressure gauge (port engine)
32 Cylinder temperature gauge (port engine)
33 Suction gauge
34 Engine speed indicator P&S

35 Undercarriage position indicator
36 Flaps position indicator
37 Cylinder temperature gauge (starboard engine)
38 Boost pressure gauge (starboard engine)
39 Starter push switch (starboard engine)
40 Wheel brake system triple air pressure gauge
41 Fire extinguisher shrouded push switches P&S
42 Oxygen regulator unit
43 Air temperature gauge
44 Undercarriage hydraulic system pressure gauge
45 Call lamp and switch

The following are only fitted in dual-control training aircraft:

46 2nd pilot's control yoke
47 2nd pilot's rudder bar
48 2nd pilot's control column

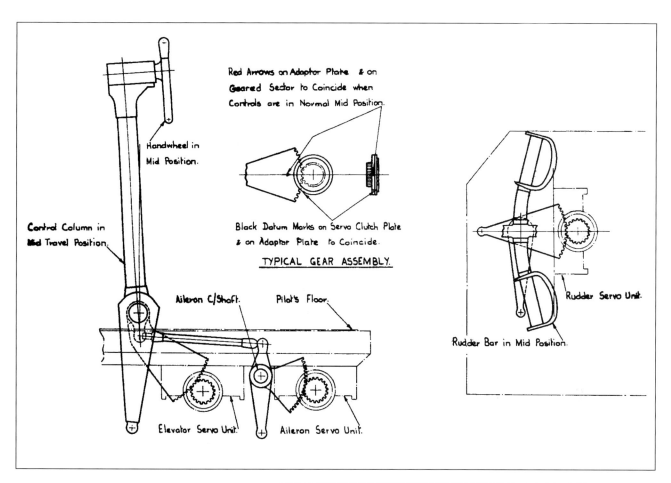

Red Arrows on Adaptor Plate & on Geared Sector to Coincide when Controls are in Normal Mid Position.

Handwheel in Mid Position.

Control Column in Mid Travel Position.

Black Datum Marks on Servo Clutch Plate & on Adaptor Plate to Coincide.

TYPICAL GEAR ASSEMBLY.

Aileron C/Shaft.

Pilot's Floor.

Elevator Servo Unit.

Aileron Servo Unit.

Rudder Servo Unit.

Rudder Bar in Mid Position.

ABOVE The Mk VIII autopilot servos engaged directly with the pilot's controls. *(Crown Copyright via The National Archives)*

the slide; the range of movement is limited by a slotted stop.

Elevator and rudder trimming tabs are controlled by cables from a single unit to the left of the pilot's seat, rotation of the spindle operating the rudder tab, and fore-and-aft movement operating the elevator tabs; fine elevator adjustments can be made via a star wheel at the side of the unit. The port aileron trimming tab is controlled by a lever to the left.

The second pilot's seat is above the bomb aimer's compartment, and hinges down on the starboard side to allow ingress and egress through the cockpit. Both pilot's seats are unpadded, as they sit on their parachutes.

RIGHT The pilot's rudder bar and pedals. The star wheel adjusts the bar for reach. *(Author)*

ABOVE The wing root at the leading edge frame, showing the push rods for controlling the engine. *(Author)*

ABOVE RIGHT The rear of the trailing edge frame with the control rod for the starboard aileron. The wide tube on the rear of the frame is the balance jack for the flaps. *(Author)*

RIGHT Detail of the aileron push rod junction at the trailing edge frame. The Elsan toilet is on the left. *(Author)*

CENTRE RIGHT Just aft of the tail frames, the elevator push rod attaches to a horn that rotates the tube to move the elevators. *(Author)*

RIGHT Looking forwards from the rear turret. *(Author)*

ABOVE LEFT The throw arm on the bottom of the rudder tube connects to the rudder push rod (entering from bottom). *(Author)*

ABOVE Detail of the trim cables for the starboard elevator passing around the frame and out into the horizontal stabiliser. Note also the connection of the stabiliser to the frame. *(Author)*

LEFT Detail of the control rods and trim cables entering the stern frame. *(Author)*

BELOW LEFT Detail of the pilot's sliding window and the front of the side window strip. *(Author)*

BELOW The pilot's seat. The hole in the backrest is for the pilot's harness, and the lever with the white knob operates an emergency hydraulic pump. *(Author)*

Turrets

The Wellington usually carries two hydraulically operated gun turrets in the nose and tail, powered by a pump connected to the port engine. The main turret configurations are as follows (all guns are .303 Browning machine guns):

- Mk I: Vickers turrets nose (one gun) and tail (two guns).
- Mk IA: Frazer-Nash FN.5 nose (two guns) and tail (two guns), FN.25 ventral (two guns).
- Mk IC, II: Frazer-Nash FN.5 nose (two guns) and tail (two guns).
- Mk III and IV (early): Frazer-Nash FN.5 nose (two guns) and FN.4 tail (four guns).
- Mk III and IV (late), X: Frazer-Nash FN.5 nose (two guns) and FN.20A/FN.120/FN.121 tail (four guns).
- Mk VIII, XI, XII, XIII, XIV: Frazer-Nash FN.20A/FN.120/FN.121 tail (four guns) – some VIIIs and XIIIs also had FN.5 nose (two guns)

Some Mk VIIIs, XIIs, and XIVs carry the unarmed FN.77 ventral turret with Leigh Light.

Some aircraft also carry additional single guns aimed manually from beam and/or nose positions and the astro-hatch.

The turrets are mounted on the terminal rings on the ends of the fuselage. For the Frazer-Nash turrets, this comprises a horizontal plate at the level of the lower longerons, propped underneath and with a hole into which the turret is fitted. The underside of the plate is covered with an aerodynamic underpan. The turrets must be correctly positioned with respect to the fuselage. It is not practicable to use a jig for this, as each aircraft settles into its own shape. Hence, each turret must be fitted and adjusted by hand; this is done on the production line by just two men. The forward underpan carries the forward identification light, and behind the front terminal ring is an immersion switch that automatically inflates the bomb bay flotation bags. Most turrets are fitted with a Mk III reflector gunsight.

Vickers turrets

Powered turrets of Vickers design are installed in the Mk I, consisting of three main assemblies: a stationary base, the gun pillar, and the sight

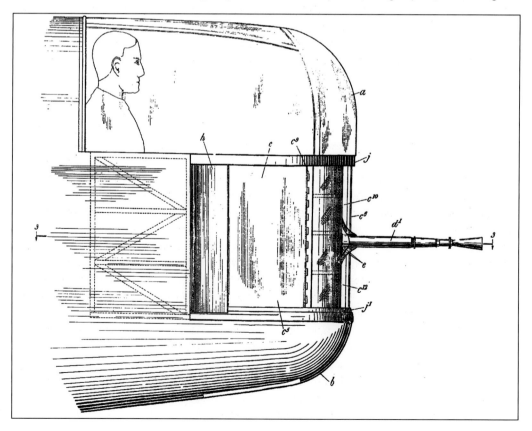

RIGHT Patent drawing of the Vickers tail turret. *(BAE Systems)*

SIGHT ARM

SIGHT HOUSING

BRACKETS FOR AMMUNITION CHUTES

CONTROL HANDLES

2 BROWNING .303 in. GUNS (REAR TURRET)

LOADING TRAY ATTACHMENT

LINK CHUTE

ROTATION CUT OFF DRIVE

STATIONARY BASE

ABOVE Main components of the Vickers turret. *(Crown Copyright via The National Archives)*

mechanism. The base is attached to the airframe and houses a Frazer-Nash control column, a Palmer hydraulic firing control mechanism, and the rotation motor that turns the gun pillar via a worm gear. The pillar is a hollow casting housing the gun elevating ram and the gun itself, as well as the sighting mechanism. Externally, the top of the turret has a fixed transparent Perspex cupola and the bottom has a movable shutter screen of metal panels that can be rotated in the manner of a roll-top desk. The guns protrude through holes in the shutter panels. Nose and tail turrets are the same, apart from the number of guns and the sealing panels (rubber in the nose and metal in the tail).

The guns are elevated by hydraulic rams and traversed by hydraulic motors (both powered by an engine-driven pump, taking approximately 6sec to traverse fully and 3sec to elevate fully) but the gunner's seat does not move. Manual turning gear is provided for emergency use. The guns are mounted at approximately knee height and gearing ensures that the gunsight movement is coordinated with the guns.

Ammunition (1,200 rounds for the nose gun and 2,000 rounds for each tail gun) is stored in boxes in the airframe and is fed through chutes to the guns, empty cartridges and belt links being discharged on to the turret floor (a thick leather washer preventing these from falling into working parts). A door in the floor of the tail turret can be opened by a pedal to discharge cartridges, but the nose turret requires a detachable panel to be unscrewed.

The Vickers turrets were considered 'wrong in design' by A&AEE and they were unpopular in service. Sighting was awkward, ammunition feeds were prone to jamming and breaking the feed chutes, and the spent shell cases could also cause jams.

Ventral turrets

The original ventral turret earmarked for the Wellington was also of Vickers design, but the Air Ministry preferred the Frazer-Nash FN.9. This turret was fitted to the first Mk I, L4212, but concerns about the effect of its weight on the centre of gravity meant that other Mk I aircraft were not equipped with it. The Vickers ventral turret was probably never fitted.

The FN.9 did not go into mass production, but was replaced by the FN.25, which is fitted to the Mk IA and early ICs. The turret is mounted between two additional wishbone ribs fitted just aft of the bomb bay, and hydraulic rams lower it through a circular opening in the bottom of the aircraft; an additional pump is provided on the starboard engine to supply power. A hand pump can be used to raise or lower the turret in an emergency, and manual rotation gear is also fitted; the turret must be

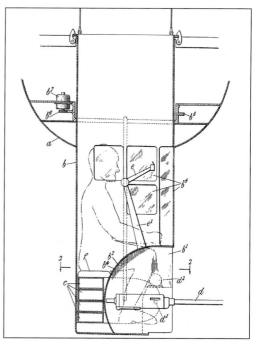

retracted for landing, and can only be partly extended with the aircraft on the ground, unless a servicing pit is used. A retractable footwell is fitted in the floor.

Although offering 360° coverage, with 50° depression and 5° elevation, the ventral 'dustbin' turret proved unsuccessful – it is heavy (around 1,500lb), the gunner's view is very restricted by the small windows (lessening its effectiveness), and its drag reduces the aircraft's speed by around 15mph at times when maximum speed is required. It is also not unknown for gunners to shoot out their own tyres!

Hence from Mk IC aircraft onwards, the ventral turret is no longer fitted, although the circular fuselage fitting is retained (being used

Looking rearwards from the trailing edge frame, with the flare chute (left), and Elsan toilet (right). Note the two wishbone frames for the deleted ventral turret. *(Author)*

for other purposes as described elsewhere). Beam protection is then provided by two single Vickers K guns (drum-fed) or Brownings (belt-fed from boxes on the floor) gimbal-mounted in glazed areas in the rear fuselage.

Frazer-Nash turrets

From the Mk IA onwards, an FN.5 two-gun nose turret is carried, which is also used as the tail turret up to the Mk II. Ammunition is carried in boxes fitted inside the turret (one for each gun with 1,000 rounds); an additional 1,000 rounds per turret is carried in the fuselage. Turret traverse is ± 95° with 60° elevation and 45° depression. By cutting back the aerodynamic fairing around the turret, traverse can be increased to ± 110°. Spent cartridges are jettisoned from the rear turret, but the front turret retains them to prevent engine ingestion.

To increase firepower in the stern of the

LEFT The rear of the front FN.5A turret with doors closed. The inside bulkhead door is not fitted. *(Author)*

BELOW The front gunner's view entering his turret, showing the spring-loaded doors. *(Author)*

BELOW Looking into the rear turret. The turret doors are not present, and the red bar is to lock the turret in position. *(Author)*

LEFT The inside of the front turret. Details are the same as the rear turret. *(Author)*

BELOW Main features of the rear turret. *(Author)*

1 Seat with canvas harness
2 Handle for manual rotation of turret
3 Handle for seat height adjustment P&S
4 Bolt-on lid of ammunition tank P&S
5 Ammunition tanks P&S
6 Plunger to lock rotation
7 Hydraulic rams to elevate/depress the guns P&S
8 Trailing intercom socket
9 Control handles P&S
10 Firing button P&S
11 Light dimmer
12 .303 Browning machine guns P&S
13 Cocking studs P&S
14 Top of ammunition feed chute
15 Mk III reflector gunsight

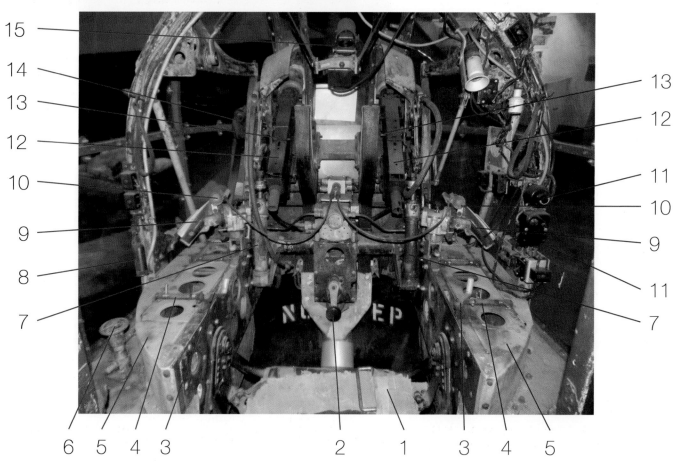

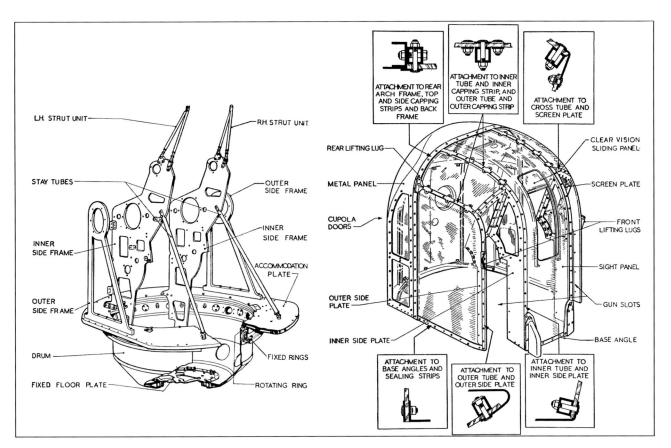

Diagram labels (left illustration):

LH. STRUT UNIT — RH. STRUT UNIT

STAY TUBES — OUTER SIDE FRAME

INNER SIDE FRAME — INNER SIDE FRAME

OUTER SIDE FRAME — ACCOMMODATION PLATE

DRUM — FIXED RINGS

FIXED FLOOR PLATE — ROTATING RING

Diagram labels (right illustration):

ATTACHMENT TO REAR ARCH FRAME, TOP AND SIDE CAPPING STRIPS AND BACK FRAME

ATTACHMENT TO INNER TUBE AND INNER CAPPING STRIP, AND OUTER TUBE AND OUTER CAPPING STRIP

ATTACHMENT TO CROSS TUBE AND SCREEN PLATE

REAR LIFTING LUG — CLEAR VISION SLIDING PANEL

METAL PANEL — SCREEN PLATE

CUPOLA DOORS — FRONT LIFTING LUGS

SIGHT PANEL

OUTER SIDE PLATE — GUN SLOTS

INNER SIDE PLATE — BASE ANGLE

ATTACHMENT TO BASE ANGLES AND SEALING STRIPS

ATTACHMENT TO OUTER TUBE AND OUTER SIDE PLATE

ATTACHMENT TO INNER TUBE AND INNER SIDE PLATE

aircraft, four-gun turrets are used. Plans to fit FN.10 tail turrets were abandoned in favour of the FN.4A turret for early Mk IIIs and IVs, but this was quickly superseded by the FN.20A, and subsequently the structurally similar FN.120 (which uses hydraulic servos to feed ammunition) and ultimately the FN.121 (which uses electric feed servos and adds a gyroscopic gunsight).

These Fraser-Nash turrets consist of the turret ring, turret drum, and superstructure. The turret ring has a fixed ring (bolted to the airframe), a gear ring (secured to the lower part of the fixed ring and engaged by the pinions of the hydraulic rotation motor and the hand rotation gear), and a rotating ring with 16 vertical and 16 horizontal rollers, which carry the weight of the turret and side forces. The turret drum is bolted to the rotating ring and has a two-part floor, the central part being fixed and carrying the services and ammunition guides. The superstructure frame consists of an accommodation plate and two inner and outer side frames, to which all other turret components are attached.

The gun cradles each carry two Browning guns, and pivot between the inner and outer frames of the superstructure. Cartridge guides feed the ammunition belts into the guns, and chutes in the base allow empty cartridges and belt links to be ejected to the rear. Sight arms are connected to the gun cradles by

ABOVE The chassis and cupola of the four-gun Frazer-Nash turrets. *(Crown Copyright via The National Archives)*

LEFT The distinguished 'chin' of 'R for Robert' carries the FN.5 nose turret and the bow navigation light. *(Author)*

linkages, so that cradle movement causes a corresponding movement of the gunsight.

The cupola is a metal-framed transparent Perspex cover protecting the gunner from the airstream, and is bolted to the accommodation plate and side frames. The rear of the cupola is solid and contains the sliding entrance doors.

The direct column carries two handles that control the rotation of the turret (by rotation of the column about its vertical axis) and elevation of the guns (by tilting the column about its horizontal axis). The turret is rotated by a hydraulic motor bolted to the right-hand side of the turret-rotating ring, a pinion engaging with a ring gear. Movement of the rotation control in one direction causes hydraulic fluid to enter the motor, causing it to rotate; movement in the other direction

causes flow in the opposite direction and hence opposite rotation of the motor. Each handle also incorporates a firing trigger that operates the sear release hydraulic rams to fire the guns.

If power is not available, the turret can be rotated from inside by means of hand rotation gear. An external rotation valve in the hydraulic supply line permits the turret to be rotated from within the airframe in an emergency. A rotation lock, consisting of a spring-loaded roller plunger, is mounted on the left side of the turret, and when depressed it locks the turret in the fore-and-aft position.

Ammunition (typically 2,000 rounds per gun) is belt-fed into the turret via ducts from four boxes within the airframe, two on each side. A servo feed provides the necessary power to pull the ammunition belts up to the guns from their storage boxes.

Electrical services to the turret include an intercom circuit, call light, and gunsight power. Cables for these services are led through a hole in the drum floor from a distributor panel in the airframe adjacent to the turret. An oxygen supply for the gunner is also connected through the drum floor.

Main systems

Fuel system

Two three-part light alloy fuel tanks are stored in each outer wing, one tank ahead of and one aft of the main spar. These carry 150 and 167

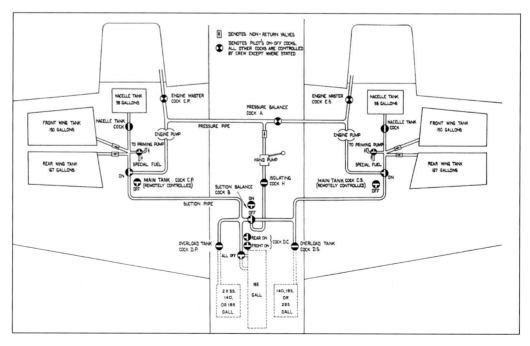

RIGHT **Fuel system schematic.** *(Crown Copyright)*

gallons, a total of 634 gallons. Each nacelle additionally carries a 58-gallon tank, usually used as an emergency tank and operated by pulling cables located adjacent to the main tank cock handles. When activated, these give approximately one hour's running time. Each engine is supplied by its own fuel pump. A hand pump mounted immediately after the main spar can be used to pressurise the system in case of pump failure. Normally, each side of the fuel system is independent, but a balance cock can be opened to connect both sides together in an emergency.

Up to three 55-, 140- or 185-gallon overload tanks can be carried in the bomb bay in place of bombs, to give up to 17 hours' endurance. Type 423 aircraft can carry a single 295-gallon tank in the bomb bay instead of bombs.

Each tank (or tank group) is filled separately. To avoid overfilling, the fuel gauges on the electrical control panel in the fuselage must be consulted during filling. The three cells of each wing tank are filled from the outboard cell, accessed via a hinged door on the wing upper surface. Nacelle tank fillers are on their top face. Outboard overload tank fillers are on the forward end, accessible through bomb compartment doors; centre cell tank fillers are on top of the tank at the forward end, accessed through a hole in the floor of the wireless operator's station, the fuel hose being

passed up through the main hatch. The pilot's fuel gauges must be activated by pressing a pushbutton above the fuel gauge on the instrument panel; there are no fuel gauges for the nacelle tanks or bomb bay overload tanks.

In an emergency, the wing fuel tanks can be emptied via discharge pipes on the underside of the wings – the pipes extend past the trailing edge flaps and incorporate a bellows to allow them to bend when the flaps are lowered. Pneumatic jettison valves are fitted in both the front and rear tanks (except Mk I aircraft); these use a strong spring to hold the valve closed,

ABOVE The connection of the outer wing to the starboard nacelle. The fuel tanks can be seen inside the wing. *(Author)*

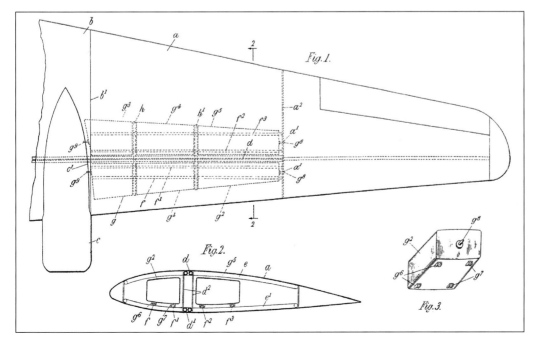

LEFT Patent drawing of the wing fuel tanks, grouped around the main spar. *(BAE Systems)*

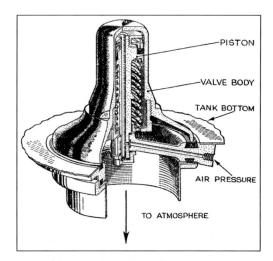

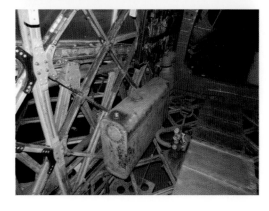

and jettison is effected by a valve on the left side of the pilot's instrument panel, which feeds compressed air into the jettison valve and forces it open against the spring.

The main fuel tanks are attached to spanwise rails inside the geodetic panels, allowing each tank group to be easily removed from the wing cell once the outer wing has been detached from the nacelle. Originally, tanks were not self-sealing, but early operational experience led to a soft rubber self-sealing cover being placed around each tank (including retro-fitting existing aircraft). This adds some 400lb to the all-up weight but, as the wing slinging points remain unchanged, weights (metal or human) have to be used to balance the wing when fitting. Armour plating was originally used only in the starboard wing but German fighter pilots quickly learned to attack the port wing, and by early 1940, all aircraft had armour in both wings.

If an engine has been unused for more than one week, carburettor priming is required, the hand pump being operated for three double strokes (or six if the float chamber is known to be empty). Throttle levers must not be moved when the engines are stopped as this might flood the cylinders with fuel.

Oil system

Main 16-gallon oil tanks are attached to the front face of the nacelle fuel tanks, and are filled through the cap on top, or replenished in flight from a 15-gallon auxiliary oil tank carried on the starboard side aft of the spar, using a hand pump (one gallon per 24 pumps); low oil levels in the nacelle tanks illuminate warning lights in the cockpit. Pumping is performed as required, usually by the second pilot (in *The Lion has Wings* he remarks: 'That's all a second pilot is for!'). Pegasus engines in particular use a lot of oil. An oil dilution system is provided to thin the oil to facilitate engine starting in cold weather.

Hydraulic system

Hydraulic pressure at 1,300psi is provided by two Vickers pumps on the port engine, one supplying the front and rear turrets, the other for all other services, such as bomb bay doors and undercarriage. Ventral turrets are supplied by an additional pump on the starboard engine (Mk IA) or port engine (Mk XII and XIV). Loss of the

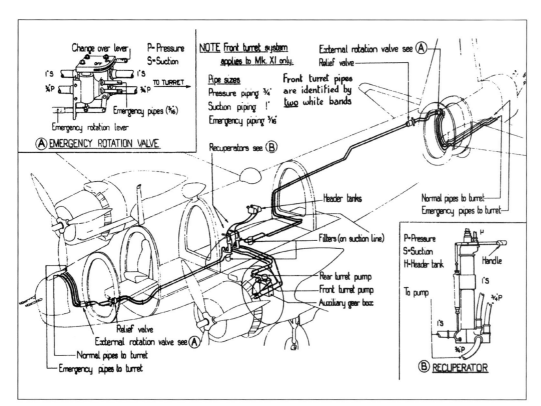

port engine typically results in the undercarriage, flaps, and bomb doors all coming down as they are held up by hydraulic pressure. A hand pump is fitted to the right of the pilot's seat for operation of flaps, undercarriage and bomb doors during servicing or in an emergency.

Recuperators in the central fuselage are incorporated in the turret hydraulic system, and act as chambers of variable volume to compensate for volume differences caused by temperature changes and by operation of the hydraulic services, as well as acting as an oil reservoir to replenish small losses. A 1.5-gallon hydraulic header tank is mounted in the wireless operator's compartment above the radio equipment.

Pneumatic system

Pneumatic pressure is provided by two compressors on the starboard engine, an RAE compressor supplying the autopilot and a BTH/AV compressor for the brakes and other services. Two cylinders in the starboard inner wing store the air at 200psi. There is a suction pump on each engine, one for the blind flying panel and the other spare.

Oxygen system

Oxygen for the crew to breathe at altitude is stored in a bank of 15 or 16 750-litre cylinders attached to the cabin roof in the mid-fuselage. Each crewmember has a Mk VIII regulator and repeater oxygen gauge, in addition to the main gauge on the pilot's instrument panel.

LEFT Behind the leading edge frame, with corroded turret hydraulic recuperators (left) and batteries (centre). *(Author)*

LEFT The roof of the mid fuselage, showing the crew oxygen cylinders and astrodome. *(Author)*

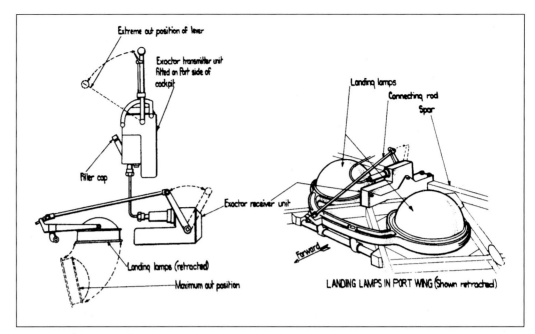

Extreme out position of lever

Exactor transmitter unit
fitted on Port side of
cockpit

Filler cap

Landing lamps (retracted)

Maximum out position

Landing lamps

Connecting rod

Spar

Exactor receiver unit

Forward

LANDING LAMPS IN PORT WING (Shown retracted)

Electrical system

Electrical generators on the starboard (or
later, both) engines provide electrical power
at 12V (Mk I and IA) or 24V (other marks);
capacity was initially 500W, expanded later
to 1,500W. 40 Ahr batteries are carried in
the mid-fuselage.

Lights with switches and/or dimmers are
located throughout the aircraft, as is a series
of crew call lamps and switches. Two 350W
landing lights are fitted on the port outer
wing just behind the leading edge at station
19; these are retracted hydraulically when
not in use.

Cabin heating

Cabin heating is provided by a Gallay system –
water in a boiler jacket around the port engine
exhaust is turned to steam and piped to a
heat exchanger in the fresh air duct to warm
incoming air before being recycled back to
the boiler; the warmed air is then piped to the
crew stations. The effectiveness of this system
is highly variable and crews are rarely warm
enough, especially at night, even with thick
flying suits, which often ice up with the moisture
from the wearer's breath. In the Mk II, the
engine coolant is used as the heat source.

RIGHT Two retractable
landing lights are
mounted behind
the port outer wing
leading edge. (Author)

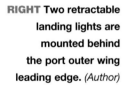

RIGHT The rear of
the two landing lights,
showing the retraction
arms. (Author)

FAR RIGHT The port
engine and nacelle;
the cloth around the
exhaust pipe is the
cover for the boiler for
cabin heating. (Author)

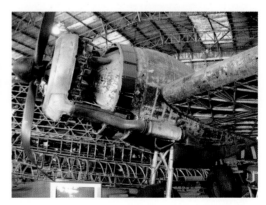

Emergency equipment

The main parachute exit is the entrance hatch beneath the cockpit, which is fitted with a foot lever at the outboard side, enabling it to be opened without using the handle. The secondary exit is a push-out panel on the lower starboard side of the fuselage midway between the wing and the tail. This is a wooden panel fitted into four 'cells' of the geodetics at station 67, and is covered with a wooden guard attached to the structure by means of press-studs.

Nine internal stowage points are available for parachutes or single dinghies.

A Graviner-type fire extinguisher system is fitted; either or both extinguishers can be fired electrically from switches on the right side of the instrument panel, and are also fired automatically by an impact switch in the nose. The system discharges methyl bromide extinguishant from a bottle behind the fireproof bulkhead into the carburettor air intake and into the nacelle via nozzles on a perforated pipe around the engine. Later aircraft have flame switches in the nacelles, which illuminate warning lamps on the pilot's instrument panel.

A hand fire extinguisher is also carried on the starboard side of the leading edge frame. Some marks carry extra extinguishers in the cockpit and near the rear turret. Fireman's axes, for cutting through the fuselage, are stowed aft of the navigator's seat and in the rear fuselage. Two first-aid kits are stored on the port side amidships and can be accessed internally, or externally via tear-off panels. A rest bunk is available in the centre fuselage.

The Wellington is unique for a medium bomber in carrying a set of emergency flotation bags for use if ditching. These are carried in 14 packs attached to perforated plates in the roof of the bomb bay. Inflation can be initiated manually by pulling handles mounted on the rear of the wing spar or automatically by an immersion switch mounted just aft of the forward turret. Up to 14 bags can be carried with a normal bomb load (including two 55-gallon overload tanks), and are inflated when required from three CO_2 cylinders stored in the inner main planes (one 3.7lb Mk II and one 7.25lb Mk III to starboard and one Mk III to port). If a 185-gallon overload tank is carried in the centre cell, the six bags

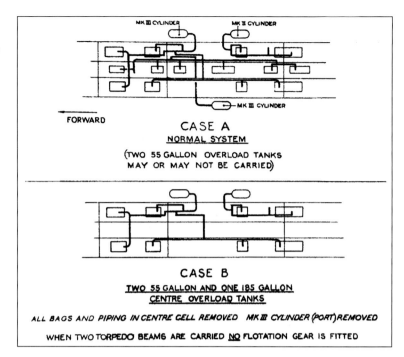

CASE A
NORMAL SYSTEM
(TWO 55 GALLON OVERLOAD TANKS MAY OR MAY NOT BE CARRIED)

CASE B
TWO 55 GALLON AND ONE 185 GALLON CENTRE OVERLOAD TANKS

ALL BAGS AND PIPING IN CENTRE CELL REMOVED   MK III CYLINDER (PORT) REMOVED

WHEN TWO TORPEDO BEAMS ARE CARRIED NO FLOTATION GEAR IS FITTED

ABOVE The flotation system, full (top) and partial (bottom). *(Crown Copyright via The National Archives)*

there (and their air cylinder) are removed. If the standard bomb beam is removed, all of the flotation gear is also taken out.

A 'J' type inflatable dinghy with accessories is carried in a container in the top of the starboard engine nacelle, and is inflated automatically by an immersion switch, or manually using handles either inside the fuselage or under a tear-off patch on the wing aft of the main spar. Emergency survival packs and a dinghy radio are carried in the fuselage, and a small box kite is packed with the dinghy to carry the aerial aloft.

Wireless operator's station

Early Wellingtons are fitted with a Marconi R1082 receiver and T1083 transmitter for voice and W/T communications. The R1082 is a tuned radio-frequency receiver with a range of 111kHz–15MHz, and the T1083 is a master oscillator-controlled transmitter with ranges of 136–500kHz and 1.5–15MHz. Frequency bands are selected using interchangeable coils, within-band tuning is then by dial.

On the floor behind the wireless operator's seat is a box containing a short-range TR9 transceiver with a frequency range of 4.3–6.6MHz. This is the standard device (in the early war period) to allow pilots to communicate with the control tower. The T1083 is for long-range

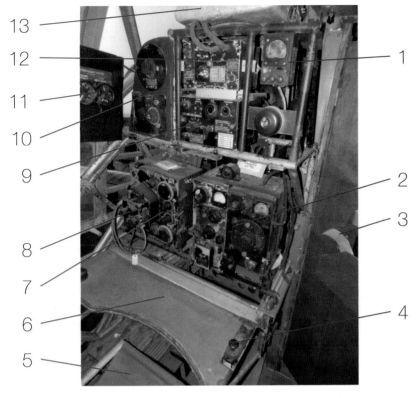

13
12
11
10
9
8
7
6
5

1 Ammeter showing current to aerial
2 T1083 transmitter unit
3 Door to cockpit with emergency axe
4 Morse key
5 Wireless operator's seat (TR9 unit behind)
6 Wireless operator's desk
7 R1082 receiver unit
8 DF loop attachment on receiver
9 Crystal calibrator to check frequencies
10 Transmitter coil unit
11 Oxygen system repeater gauges
12 A1134 amplifier for crew intercom
13 Hydraulic system header tank

1
2
3
4

use only, but can be used as a back-up for the TR9 if required. In later aircraft, a VHF set replaces the TR9.

The Wellington is also fitted with an A1134 audio frequency amplifier for crew communication within the aircraft, which is interconnected with the TR9.

From 1941, the R1082/T0183 was replaced by the Marconi R1155/T1154 – the R1155 superheterodyne receiver has five switch-selected frequency bands across the range 75kHz–18.5MHz with a direction finding (DF) and homing capability, and the T1154 is a master oscillator-controlled transmitter with a similar range in four switched bands. Voice communication is limited to around ten miles; W/T is used for longer range. The R1155/T1154 remained standard in all large RAF aircraft until after the war. Additional radio equipment is carried by later marks.

All radios are powered by rotary transformer units running from the aircraft batteries.

RIGHT Behind the wireless operator's seat is the TR9 transceiver for short-range air-to-ground communication. *(Author)*

FAR RIGHT The reel just above the longeron is for the 200ft trailing radio aerial. *(Author)*

The main radio aerial is fitted between two masts on the fuselage roof (early aircraft), or between a forward mast and the fin. The TR9 aerial exits via the roof of the compartment and is clipped on to the main aerial. To improve medium frequency signal reception, a 200ft trailing aerial (weighted with twenty ½in lead balls) can be extended from a reel on the port rear fuselage. This is deployed when in flight and must be reeled back in before landing.

A DF loop is carried on the roof of the navigator's station to enable the wireless operator to gauge the bearing of incoming radio signals; the loop can be rotated remotely by the wireless operator from his seat. On all but very early aircraft, the loop has a moulded Perspex teardrop-shaped aerodynamic cover. A Morse key is fitted to the right side of the wireless operator's table.

From the Mk IA onwards, an armoured bulkhead is provided aft of the wireless operator's position to protect him and the pilot from gunfire from astern. From the IC onwards, a Lorenz blind approach system is fitted, with its 'handrail' aerial beneath the rear fuselage. Later aircraft are fitted with an Identification Friend or Foe (IFF) system, with aerials extending from the fuselage sides to the tips of the horizontal stabilisers.

A signal pistol, with eight cartridges, is stored in the roof of the compartment.

ABOVE Along the fuselage top are (from left) the aerial mast, DF loop in teardrop fairing, and astrodome. The stub fin is for the TR9 aerial, which connects on to the main aerial. *(Author)*

LEFT The wireless operator's seat with the armour bulkhead separating him from the navigator. *(Author)*

LEFT The wireless operator's instrument panel. From left: clock; altimeter; ASI; DF loop position (lamp above with dimmer below); oxygen gauges. *(Author)*

RIGHT Wireless operator's compartment, with instruments (left) and radio equipment ahead of his table. The prominent white disc is for the DF loop. *(Author)*

RIGHT The 1½-gallon hydraulic header tank above the wireless equipment. *(Author)*

FAR RIGHT The wireless operator's table, with Morse key on the right. The hole in the floor was used to fill the overload tank in the bomb bay beneath. *(Author)*

RIGHT The wireless operator's compartment in the Brooklands walk-through exhibit, which shows the later T1154/R1155 radio equipment. *(Author)*

FAR RIGHT Inside the rear fuselage, with the tail control pushrods and trim cables on the left. *(Author)*

FAR LEFT The navigator's chair and table (with map storage beneath). (Author)

LEFT The navigator's station, with its lamp and map-plotting arm. Note the curtain rail above the side window, the blue compass, and (above) clock and oxygen gauges. (Author)

LEFT Roof of the navigator's station showing the base of the DF loop and the map table lamp. (Author)

Navigator's station

The navigator's station is immediately aft of the wireless operator's station, also on the port side. His table is fixed and his seat slides in transverse runners so that it can be pushed under the table when not in use; no seatbelt anchorages are provided.

A transparent Perspex astrodome is provided on the roof of the fuselage for use as a lookout and for taking sextant readings. On early aircraft, a sliding hatch is fitted instead, which can also be used to mount a manually operated gun when required. A pedestal underneath gives the user sufficient height for a good view; a safety harness anchorage point is provided. The navigator and wireless operator stations are fitted with sound insulation.

LEFT The view aft from the astrodome. The 'Wellington' against the wall is the walk-though exhibit made from the original mid-section of 'R for Robert'. (Author)

LEFT On the left of the bomb aimer's compartment is a downward-facing F.24 camera for taking aiming point photos. *(Author)*

Bomb aimer's station

The bomb aimer's compartment occupies the lower fuselage between the front turret and the cockpit. It has three downward-looking glazed panels and, on early aircraft, a vector Course Setting Bombsight (CSBS) Mk VIIA is fitted, which was operated manually with the bomb aimer prone on a mattress. The CSBS was superseded by the Mk XIV vector bombsight with its mechanical computer and separate sighting head; this requires compressed air, suction, and electrical power. An instrument panel on the starboard side of

LEFT The panel on the right of the bomb aimer's compartment includes the bombing master switch, selector, fusing switches, and release button. *(Author)*

BELOW LEFT The Course Setting Bombsight in the nose, with the base of the bow turret above. *(Author)*

BELOW The Venturi tube beneath the bomb aimer's compartment provides suction for the artificial horizon instrument. *(Author)*

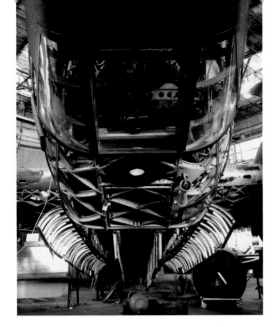

ABOVE Underside of the nose, showing (from top): the bombsight; downward identification light; main hatch (closed); and bomb bay. *(Author)*

the compartment holds the bomb distributor panel and other controls. A camera for target photography is mounted on the port side.

Externally, a downward-pointing identification lamp (red, green, and amber lamps on later aircraft) is fitted ahead of the hatch, controlled by a dashboard switch including a Morse key, and a Venturi mounted beside the entrance hatch provides suction for the artificial horizon instrument.

Pyrotechnics

Racks on the starboard side carry from three to eleven reconnaissance flares. These are launched through the flare chute, which is fitted with a draught-excluding lid and a retractable guide for shielding the flare from the airstream until it is clear of the aircraft. Flare launching procedure is as follows:

- Open lid of the chute, release the guide-locking handwheel and extend the guide, then re-lock with the handwheel.
- Place flare tail-first in the chute and secure the catch.
- Unwind the fusing cable and attach to the fusing pin in the nose.
- Release the flare by pulling the catch handle.
- Reset the catch and wind in the fusing cable.

Some marks are fitted with additional flare chutes in the ventral fitting; their release is

ABOVE The main flare chute exits just aft of the starboard wing. The rail inside could be extended to carry the flare away from the aircraft before being released into the slipstream. *(Author)*

LEFT Looking up the flare chute behind the starboard wing. *(Author)*

BELOW The top of the main flare chute. Pyrotechnics are stored in the metal chest beneath. *(Author)*

controlled by the bomb aimer. Flame floats and sea markers are carried by some marks, and launched via the flare chute. Reconnaissance flares can also be carried in the bomb bay. The flare chute is also used for dropping propaganda leaflets during 'nickel' operations. Aircraft prior to Mk IIIs have two emergency flare launchers in the port inner wing.

Care must be taken when dropping photo-flashes as they can get stuck if placed in the chute incorrectly, and if they ignite in the tube, they can blow off the tail of the aircraft.

Ground handling

The aircraft can be towed forwards using a bridle attached to the inboard axle bearings while being steered using a tail wheel steering arm, or towed backwards using the same steering arm. The arm incorporates a trip that disconnects it if excessive loads are encountered. Cover sets are provided to suit cockpit windows, turrets, and engines.

RIGHT The FN.77 turret with Leigh Light. It fitted in place of the redundant ventral gun turret. *(Crown Copyright via The National Archives)*

Tropicalisation

Special modifications are carried out on aircraft operating in tropical climates. These include additional air filters (especially important in desert areas), oil coolers, gaiters for shock absorbers, and extra emergency food and water rations. Regular checks of the covering are also required as sunlight reduces the life of the fabric.

Coastal Command equipment

Leigh Light

The original Leigh Light was a 20in Admiralty Pattern carbon arc searchlight with a 24in parabolic reflector producing a 4° divergent beam. Later versions use a lens to spread the beam to 12° to make it easier to acquire the target. The light is built into a Frazer-Nash FN.77 retractable ventral turret, a modified version of the FN.25 gun turret. The turret cylinder and hydraulics are manufactured by Parnall Aircraft (and W. Hooper of Birmingham), and the lights fitted by the Carlisle Electric Co. and Savage & Parsons of Watford.

The light can be steered hydraulically both in azimuth and elevation (usually by the second pilot) from the nose. Two electrically operated dials indicate the depression and azimuth angles, allowing the lamp to be positioned before being switched on. Azimuth movement is restricted to 180° left and 60° right, with a maximum speed of 50° per second, operated by a hand control of the same type as in the Frazer-Nash gun turrets.

The beam is powerful enough to illuminate a U-boat two miles away from 2,000ft, but in practice the light is normally switched on at around ¾ mile from the target, at a height of 50–100ft. Radio altimeters are used to maintain height at low level.

Although the trials Wellington had used the DWI generator set mounted in the fuselage, it was found more practical to power the lamp from a battery pack of the type used by the Turbinlite, which was initially located in the centre bomb cell, taking the place of two of the six depth charges (the outer cells each carry a 140-gallon overload tank for maximum

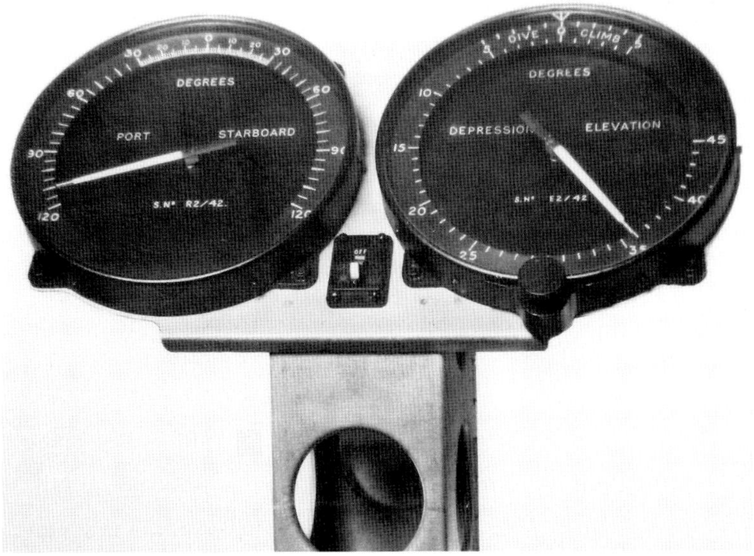

RIGHT Gauges in the nose control position allowed the light to be positioned as required before being switched on. *(Crown Copyright via The National Archives)*

range). Seven standard 12V accumulators are used to supply 100–150 amps at 75 volts to the light to give around six minutes of continuous use, and are recharged by a generator driven by the port engine. With the Leigh Light aft of the wing and no nose turret, this configuration was rather tail heavy, so the batteries were moved to the lower nose, and a mattress placed on top for the light operator to lie on. This modification improves aircraft handling, and also allows the original six depth charges to be carried.

Many Warwicks are fitted with the Leigh Light ventral turret as well, and other aircraft such as Catalinas and Liberators also carry the lights in a streamlined nacelle on the wing (as they have no retractable turret).

ASV Mk II

ASV Mk II radar is based on Airborne Interception (AI) Mk IV without the height detection aerials, and uses a wavelength of around 1.5m. The equipment consists of a power unit, control panel, transmitter, and receiver. Radar pulses

BELOW Schematic of the hydraulic system for lowering and controlling the Leigh Light. *(Crown Copyright via The National Archives)*

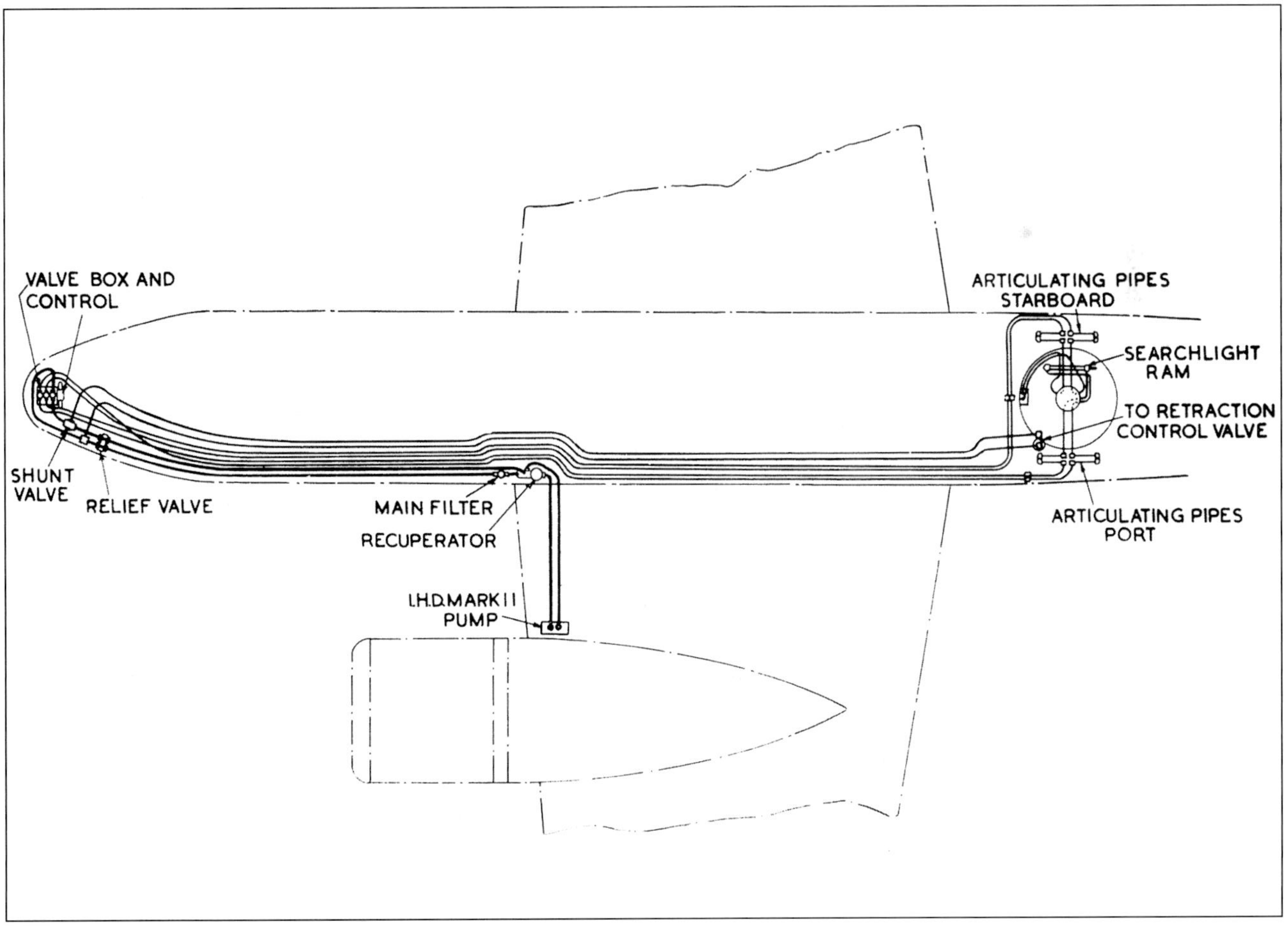

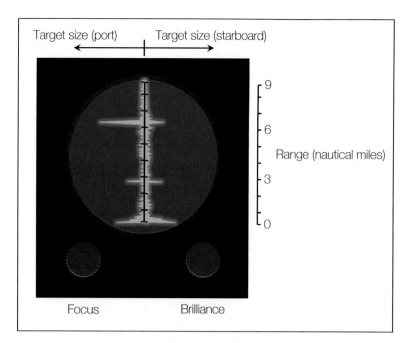

Target size (port) Target size (starboard)

9

6

Range (nautical miles)

3

0

Focus   Brilliance

ABOVE Simulation of the screen of an ASV Mk II set. There is a large target to port about seven miles distant and a smaller target straight ahead about three miles distant. The signal at the bottom of the display is short-range clutter from the sea. *(Author)*

are radiated through dipole aerials on the top and sides of the fuselage giving coverage up to 80° each side of the aircraft heading. Reflections are picked up by two Yagi aerials (similar to terrestrial TV aerials), one under each wing. The signals from the aerials are displayed on the two sides of a cathode ray tube. The relative horizontal sizes of the traces on each side of the screen centreline allow the operator to discern the direction to the target (equal traces indicate a target dead ahead), while the vertical axis

indicates range. Some aircraft have a third small Yagi beneath the nose.

Detection range increases with height up to 6,000ft and is up to 30 miles in ideal conditions, but more typically around 10 miles. Reflections from the surface of the sea give rise to clutter on the screen (at their worst at shorter ranges), through which the operator has to detect any real targets. ASV is unaffected by weather, and it can also detect land, hence it can be used to assist with navigation. It cannot, however, be used at the same time as the WT receiver.

ASV Mk III

ASV Mk III is based on the H2S navigation radar developed for Bomber Command, and uses a rotating scanner to both project and receive a narrow beam of signal pulses. Wavelength is 9.1cm (later 3cm), the scanner rotating approximately once every second. The return signal is fed to a Plan Position Indicator (PPI) screen, which in effect displays a map of the area centred on the aircraft. In H2S, the top of the PPI display is always north (whatever the aircraft heading), but in ASV Mk III the top of the display is aligned with the aircraft heading, to aid homing. All of the electronic equipment is contained in a unit 14in x 9in x 8in. The scanner is under the nose of the Wellington so that it does not obscure the Leigh Light beam.

RIGHT Interconnection of the main components of ASV Mk IIIA apparatus. *(Crown Copyright via The National Archives)*

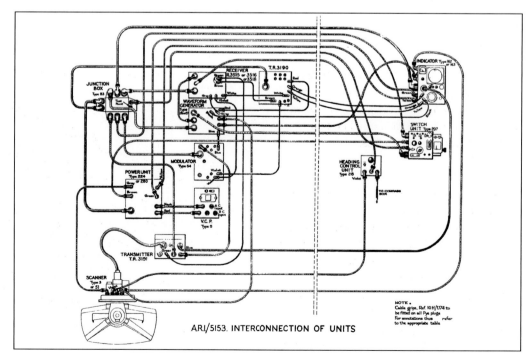

ARI/5153. INTERCONNECTION OF UNITS

Weapon loads

As a front-line bomber, the Wellington was designed to carry all of the types of bombs available to the RAF at the time – although this initially comprised only 500lb and 250lb GP and SAP bombs (plus practice bombs). A standard bomb load was thus either eighteen 250lb or nine 500lb bombs, although a mixture of sizes was often carried.

The three compartments in the bomb bay can each carry up to six bombs – three in line on the top tier and three more on the bottom tier (the top tier in the centre compartment is attached to the starboard truss, and the bottom tier to the port truss, so that both trusses carry the same load). The bomb slips are fitted within the width of the truss and hinged at the top, pivoting out to attach to the bombs. Bombs in the bottom tier are set to release first. Safety contacts prevent a bomb being released while another is still in position in the tier below.

1,000lb and 2,000lb bombs

When these larger bombs arrived, they required an additional bomb beam to be fitted in the top of the bomb bay. The bombs were attached to a carrier beam (with integral bomb slip) by a sling, and the carrier with bomb attached was winched up and secured to the bomb beam.

Rodded bombs

Rodded bombs were used for anti-personnel operations in some areas – these were standard GP bombs with long rods attached to the pistols to detonate the bomb just above ground. These were very sensitive, and there were several instances of rodded bombs causing groundcrew casualties.

Small Bomb Containers

In early 1940, the Small Bomb Container was introduced. The SBC was a lightly constructed metal box, open at the bottom, typically used to carry three canisters of 27 x 4lb stick incendiary bombs. These canisters were each held in place by hinged drop bars, which could be released electrically to drop the bombs. An adapter frame was required to carry an SBC in a Wellington, allowing it to be attached to a standard bomb slip in the same way as a 500lb

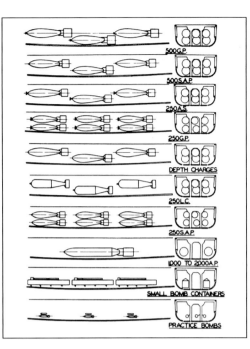

LEFT Standard bomb load options. *(Crown Copyright)*

LEFT A (dummy) 250lb bomb hung on the bomb beam. Note the bomb slip pivoted out of the beam to attach to the lug on the bomb. *(Author)*

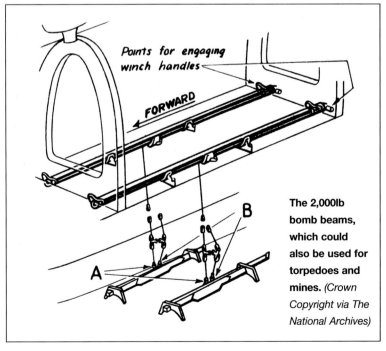

The 2,000lb bomb beams, which could also be used for torpedoes and mines. *(Crown Copyright via The National Archives)*

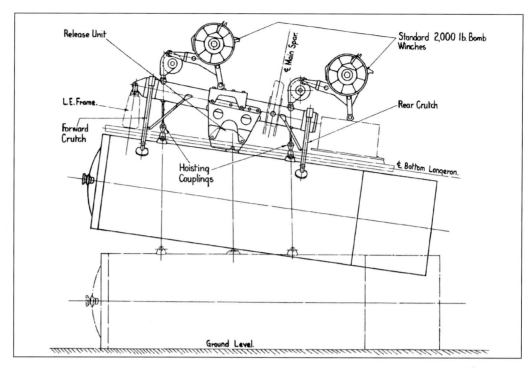

Release Unit

Standard 2,000 lb Bomb Winches

₵ Main Spar.

L.E. Frame.

Rear Crutch

Forward Crutch

Hoisting Couplings

₵ Bottom Longeron.

Ground Level.

RIGHT Loading a 4,000lb HC 'Cookie'. Note how the internal bomb beam with release unit attaches to the fuselage frames.
(Crown Copyright via Brooklands Museum)

BELOW A late-type 4,000lb HC 'Cookie' awaits loading into an aircraft of 420 (Snowy Owl) Squadron RCAF.
(Bert Parker)

bomb. The aircraft could carry up to six SBCs (in the outer bomb cells only), or fewer as part of a mixed load with conventional bombs.

4,000lb HC bombs

The 4,000lb High Capacity 'Cookie' was designed for maximum blast effect. For carriage in the Wellington, the standard bomb beam had to be removed entirely, and a new beam was installed above the bomb bay roof, attached to the leading edge frame and a new widened spar box on the centreline of the main spar. A 4,000lb Type F bomb slip was attached to this beam and positioned just above the bomb

bay roof, allowing the 'Cookie' to lie flush with the roof, with crutches attached to the beam projecting down into the bomb bay. Even in this position, the bomb still protruded a few inches below the bottom of the aircraft, so the bomb doors underneath the bomb were removed entirely, and a wooden framework was added in the bomb bay for the remaining doors to rest against. On release, the bomb simply fell through the hole.

This conversion was coded Type 423, and was applied to examples of several marks of aircraft (these aircraft were not given unique mark numbers) on the production line. Mk IIs W5389, W5399 and W5400 were the first aircraft to be converted. Often only one aircraft in a squadron would carry a 'Cookie', this aircraft taking off last in case of mishap.

500lb GP bombs account for the greatest tonnage of bombs dropped by Wellingtons (about one-third of the total tonnage), followed by 4lb incendiaries, 250lb GPs, and 4,000lb HCs.

Torpedoes

Given the shape and capacity of its bomb bay, it is surprising that torpedo-bombing was not a role that the Wellington was initially considered for. Originating as a field conversion in North Africa, the torpedo modification involved

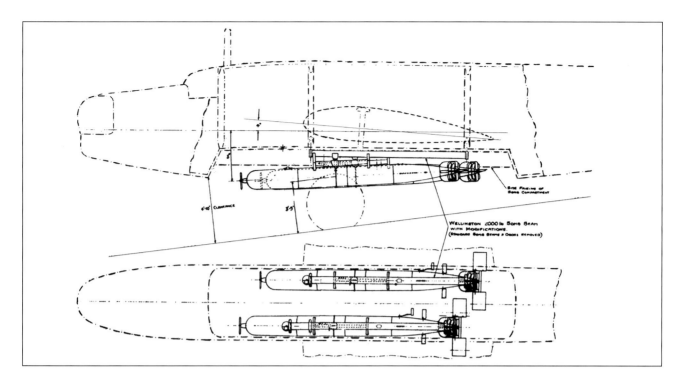

replacing the standard bomb beam with slimline beams fixed beneath the leading and trailing edge frames. The torpedoes were attached to the beams using slinged carriers, and sling retraction gear was fitted to prevent these fouling the doors after dropping.

The conversion was approved and was subsequently factory-fitted to some Coastal Command variants on the production line. Standard 18in naval torpedoes weighing 1,600lb could be carried internally. If air tails were fitted, the bomb doors were removed.

Torpedoes were loaded using the normal bomb winches and special trolleys with scissors lifting gear. Some aircraft were fitted with sighting bars ahead of the cockpit to assist in aiming the torpedoes, which were dropped by the pilot from no higher than 100ft – trainees were fined ten shillings if they dropped one too high.

Mines

British 1,500lb air-dropped sea mines were similar in shape to torpedoes, and could be carried either on standard 2,000lb bomb beams or on torpedo beams. They were loaded from torpedo trolleys or conventional bomb trolleys.

ABOVE Method of carrying two Mk XII naval torpedoes. These have air tails, hence one torpedo is slightly aft of the other. *(Crown Copyright)*

FAR LEFT Loading torpedoes (without air tails). The nose turret has been replaced by a fairing, and a sighting bar is visible ahead of the cockpit windows. *(Crown Copyright)*

LEFT Loading a sea mine into the port bomb cell. This was similar to loading a torpedo. *(Crown Copyright via The National Archives)*

Chapter Four
Engines

The Wellington principally used
Bristol radial engines, but small
numbers also used Rolls-Royce
in-line engines and Pratt &
Whitney radials.

OPPOSITE The combination of the Bristol Pegasus and the
de Havilland 'bracket-type' propellers powered about one-third
of Wellingtons. The teddy bear is a non-standard attachment.
(Crown Copyright)

Introduction

It was a mark of the Wellington's versatility that it could be fitted with a number of different engines, both radial and in-line, following the adoption of the 'power egg' concept from the Mk IC onwards. Four main engine types were employed: Bristol Pegasus on Mk I, IA, IC, and VIII; Rolls-Royce Merlin on Mk II and VI; Pratt & Whitney Twin Wasp on Mk IV; and Bristol Hercules on all other marks.

The engines were attached to the fireproof bulkhead on the front of the nacelle at six points, the Merlins via a tubular steel cradle, and the radial engines via a pair of W-frames, covered by an aerodynamic shell. Merlin cowlings consisted of detachable side, top, and bottom panels, while the radial engines had NACA cowlings with an exhaust collector ring forming the leading edge, two semi-cylindrical side access panels, and a ring of cooling gills at the rear. Merlins had short ejector exhausts directly from each pair of cylinders (three on each side, six on some Mk VIs), while the radial exhausts were pipes from the collector rings (outboard on Pegasus, inboard on Hercules and on both sides of the Twin Wasp). Port engines incorporated a boiler jacket for cabin heating, and later types had flame dampers at the rear. All aircraft were fitted with electric starters (with hand-turning back-up), power being supplied from a battery trolley plugged into a socket on the starboard side at station 23 until the engines were running.

Bristol Pegasus

The Bristol Aeroplane Company was unusual in that it not only designed and built engines for its own aircraft, but also sold these to other aircraft companies. Vickers had a long history of utilising Bristol engines in their aircraft, including the Victoria, Vildebeeste, Viastra, and Vespa – the latter setting a world altitude record with a Bristol Pegasus in 1932. The Wellesley also used the Pegasus, capturing the world distance record with it in 1938. Many other aircraft also used this engine, some of the most notable including the Handley Page Hampden, the Short Sunderland, and the Fairey Swordfish, in addition to the Wellington.

The Pegasus is a radial engine derived from the earlier Mercury and Jupiter engines. Bristol's Chief Designer, Roy Fedden, was a strong advocate of the radial engine, preferring the simplicity of direct airflow cooling of the cylinders to the complexity of the liquid cooling systems used by in-line engines, despite the higher drag of the radial layout if not properly cowled (the radial vs in-line debate for high-performance engines was never completely resolved by the time jet engines arrived). With the radial engine, a single cylinder could be removed for inspection, which was not possible with in-line engines, which were more prone to flak damage than radials.

The Pegasus was developed from its original 620hp up to 1,010hp before being superseded by the two-row engines. The 620hp Pegasus IIM.3 was used on the G.4/31 biplane, and the 690hp IIIM.3 on the monoplane prototype. The 980hp X was used on the production Wellesley and the Wellington prototype, and the long-range Wellesleys were fitted with 835hp Pegasus XXIIs, a variant specially developed for this purpose. Early production Wellingtons used the XVIII (the only Pegasus with a two-speed supercharger) developing 815hp.*

As with aircraft, many engines were built in shadow factories. These had been established in the mid-1930s at several car firms (though were owned by the government), and produced components that were then assembled either at Austin's or Bristol's factories. Bristol had long experience of licensing engine production and optimised their designs for mass production. Around 20,500 Pegasus engines of all models were built, most of which were shadow factory engines. Two Pegasus engines remain flightworthy in the UK, on the two Fairey Swordfish of the Royal Navy Historic Flight.

Note that the different mark and code suffixes to engine names often do not refer to chronological development, but may be because of small specification changes, such as supercharger gear ratios or the type of carburettor fitted. Manufacturers and the Air Ministry often used different codes for the same engine.

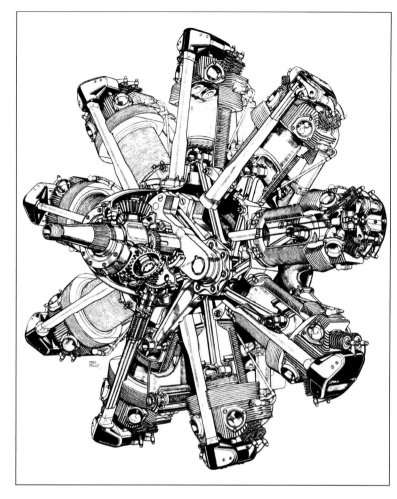

RIGHT Pegasus cutaway, showing epicyclic reduction gear, crankshaft, and pistons. *(Courtesy of* Flight International*)*

Construction

The Pegasus is a 28.7-litre, single-row, nine-cylinder, air-cooled radial engine using poppet valves, with all the connecting rods acting on one crankpin. The main elements of the engine are (from front to rear): propeller reduction gear, crankcase (with valve mechanism and cylinders), supercharger and auxiliaries (carburettor, pumps, etc.). The crankcase is in two parts, machined from aluminium alloy drop-forgings, with front and rear sections joined on the centreline of the cylinders with nickel-chrome steel bolts. A front cover is mounted on the front half crankcase and houses a cam and tappet mechanism driven from the front half of the crankshaft. The crankshaft is in two halves, the coupling being made at the rear end of the crankpin. The connecting-rod assembly comprises eight

BELOW This Pegasus preserved at Brooklands Museum was recovered from a crash site in the Western Isles. *(Author)*

BELOW Detail of the sectioned cylinder. The black bars cover the tappet mechanisms and the red discs cover the exhaust ports. *(Author)*

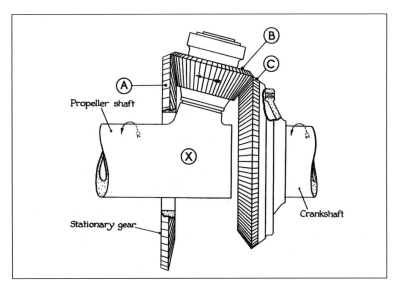

articulated rods and one master rod. Bolted to the front cover is an epicyclic reduction-gear unit driven by the nose of the crankshaft to turn the propeller at half the speed of the crankshaft while rotating on the same axis. The propeller shaft is supported at the front by a ball thrust bearing which transmits the propeller thrust to the engine crankcase and thus to the aircraft, and at the rear by a plain bush in the nose of the crankshaft. All engines rotate left-hand, i.e. anti-clockwise from the pilot's viewpoint.

The cylinder barrels are made from steel and heavily finned, while the head is forged aluminium screwed on, with a copper washer between to form a gas-tight joint. Four valve

seats of steel alloy are screwed into the head, together with valve guides and two spark plug adapters. Pistons are machined from aluminium alloy drop stampings with two gas rings and three scraper rings.

The exhaust from the cylinders passes into a collector ring mounted ahead of the cylinders, from where it is passed to a single exhaust pipe. This arrangement efficiently cools the exhaust gases in the airflow, and helps to silence and flame-damp the engine.

The carburettor combines air and fuel in the required proportions for feeding to the cylinders. A Claudel Hobson duplex master control carburettor is mounted on the intake side of the supercharger, and is of the duplex up-draught master control type, and incorporates a three-stage automatic boost control and a two-position automatic mixture control.

The oil pump is located at the port side of the rear cover and incorporates a high initial oil pressure device to supply adequate lubrication during the early stages of running after a cold start. This device automatically cuts out when the engine has warmed up.

Spark plug firing is achieved using magnetos, which use a rotating coil inside a permanent magnet to generate the required bursts of high-voltage electricity. These are universally used on piston aero engines, as they are highly reliable and require no battery. Single contact-breaker

magnetos with automatic ignition couplings are fitted to the Pegasus.

The carburettor air intake is mounted beneath the engine and has a moveable shutter to select cold or warm air. Cold air should be used for starting, ground running, when the throttle is more advanced than the maximum climbing position or when atmospheric temperature is above 15°C. Warm air should be used for all other conditions, and can also be used for take-off when icing conditions exist. An air filter is fitted to the intake to exclude dust particles. This consists of a sheet of fabric or cotton fibre supported by wire gauze across the intake path. Special filters are required for dusty environments, such as desert operation.

The Pegasus is fitted with a domed perforated plate between the propeller and the cylinders, to reduce drag while redirecting airflow from the inner part of the cylinders (which need less cooling) to maximise flow to the heads. Later engines have better baffling on the cylinders to control the cooling, so front plates are not required. Two oil-cooler inlet pipes are mounted between the cylinders at the top of the engine.

Single-engine performance with the Pegasus is marginal.

Supercharging

As an aircraft climbs, the reducing atmospheric pressure at the carburettor causes the power

ABOVE LEFT The starboard side of the port engine, showing the supports for the cooling gill ring. (Author)

ABOVE The underside of the port Pegasus, showing the air intake with its mesh filter. (Author)

LEFT The starboard engine. The panel on the fuselage (just below the carburettor air intake) covers the connections for ground starting. (Author)

output of the engine to fall. In 1916, the supercharger (or 'blower') was introduced – this uses an impeller between the carburettor and engine to compress the incoming air/fuel mixture back to sea level pressure (or higher) and hence restore the original power (less the small quantity used to drive the impeller). The amount of additional pressure generated by the supercharger (the difference between ambient pressure and the inlet manifold pressure) is known as boost. However, supercharger boost can also be used

to improve engine performance at low level, and Fedden was a pioneer in using superchargers in this way, rather than simply compensating for the effects of altitude. Conventional superchargers use gearing from the crankshaft to drive the impeller (usually with two gear ratios), while turbo-superchargers (turbochargers) use the exhaust outflow to drive it.

The supercharger can maintain its 'rated boost' up to its 'rated altitude', after which the carburettor valves are fully open and engine power starts to fall. Below the rated altitude, the engine must be throttled to prevent damage – this can lead to inefficient operation at lower levels, hence the use of two-speed superchargers that (in effect) give two different rated altitudes. The altitude at which more power can be obtained by moving the supercharger to high gear varies according to various factors, including rpm, airspeed, and atmospheric conditions. Typically, the lower gear is employed for take-off and up to 10,000ft, the higher gear being selected for maximum power, although for more efficient cruising the lower gear should remain selected as long as

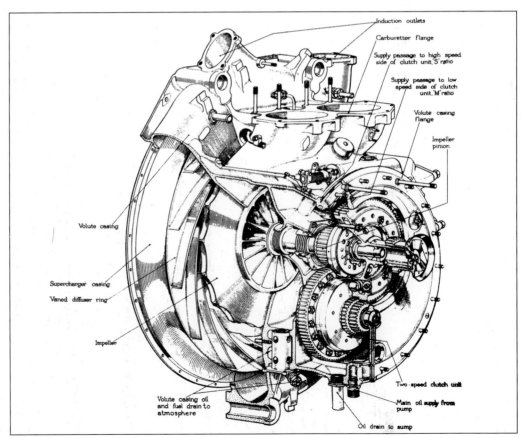

it will give the required power. Gear changes result in a momentary drop in oil pressure, which indicates that the hydraulic clutches are functioning correctly. During long flights, the supercharger gear should be changed periodically to clear any sludge built up in the clutch. This should also be done after landing before shutting down the engines.

All but very early Pegasus versions have gear-driven single-stage superchargers, some versions being single-speed and some two-speed. The nickel-chrome impeller is coaxial with the crankshaft, mounted on the rear set of crankcase bolts and driven by step-up gearing incorporating a change speed mechanism. Different gear ratios are used to optimise characteristics between take-off/low-level and high-level flight performance (e.g. Coastal Command vs Bomber Command duties). The tail shaft passes through the hollow impeller spindle to power various auxiliary drives and assemblies mounted on the rear cover of the engine, such as the electric generator, oil pump, vacuum pump, air compressor, and hydraulic pump.

For maximum range, set the throttle to the maximum economical cruise position and maintain the required airspeed by adjusting the rpm between 1,600 and the maximum permissible for economical cruising. Flight tests must be performed on the particular installation type to determine the indicated airspeed that gives the most air miles per gallon – this optimum IAS is almost constant at all altitudes but varies with the all-up weight of the aircraft.

Cooling gills

A ring of small flaps circling the rear of the engine cowling, known as gills, is used to vary the amount of cooling airflow passing through the engine, to keep the cylinder temperatures within acceptable limits. The ring is attached to the rear of the engine, and the flaps are fixed to brackets that are interconnected by a chain and sprockets, and are opened by turning a handle in the cockpit (one for each engine, clockwise to open). In general, gills should be closed as fully as possible without causing the maximum cylinder temperature to be exceeded. They must be fully open during taxiing and ground running, and not less than one-third open for take-off. When gliding or diving, they should be fully closed.

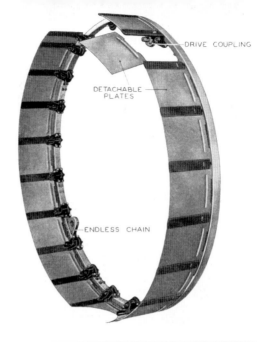

LEFT The Hercules gill ring. *(Crown Copyright)*

MAIN PARTICULARS – BRISTOL PEGASUS XVIII

Type	Single-row, nine-cylinder, poppet-valve, air-cooled radial (four valves per cylinder)
Firing order	1, 3, 5, 7, 9, 2, 4, 6, 8 (cylinders are equally spaced and numbered 1–9 clockwise starting from the top, looking from the front)
Bore/stroke	5.75in/7.5in
Swept volume	1,753cu in (28.7 litres)
Compression ratio	6.25:1
Supercharger gear ratio	6.9:1 (low gear 'M')/9.9:1 (high gear 'S')
Continuous power	815bhp at 2,250rpm
Propeller reduction gear	Bevel epicyclic 0.5:1
Diameter/length	55.3in/61in
Weight (dry)	1,140lb
Rated altitude	4,750ft ('M' gear)/14,750ft ('S' gear)
Fuel type/consumption	DED2475 (100 octane) or DTD230 (87 octane)/198 gal/hr
Oil type/normal pressure	DTD472/80psi at 70°C above 2,000rpm
Carburettor	Claudel Hobson AVT 95MB
Fuel pump pressure	9–10psi
Carburettor fuel pressure	2.5psi
Magnetos	BTH C3SE 9S (two fitted)
Spark plugs	KLG type RC12R, or Lodge type RS14/1R, or AC Sphinx type RZ14R
Starter	Eclipse E160 electric (with hand-turning equipment)
Propeller	Left-hand tractor de Havilland 20° variable-pitch, constant speed control, diameter 12ft 6in

Air Publication AP1451 gives full details of the installation, maintenance, and operation of the Pegasus.

PROPELLERS

Wellingtons are fitted with variable-pitch propellers, each blade being attached to a pivot in the hub, allowing the angle of the blade to be altered while the propeller is turning, the aim being to vary the thrust while keeping the engine speed constant at its most efficient value. The propeller control should always be moved slowly so that the change in rpm follows its movement. When making large power reductions, the throttle lever should be moved before the propeller control, and the propeller control first when increasing. For taxiing, take-off, initial climb, and combat, the propeller speed control should be set to give maximum engine rpm.

Later propellers are fitted with feathering controls, allowing the blades to be turned edge-on to the airflow for minimum drag in the case of an engine failure.

Three-bladed propellers are used on most Wellingtons, while four-bladed propellers are used on the high-altitude variants and some special conversions. Propellers on early aircraft have built-in heads that spray de-icing fluid by centrifugal force from a 6½-gallon tank in the port nacelle. De-icing 'snowdrop' grease is also used on the propellers and leading edges when required.

De Havilland variable-pitch propellers

The blades are counterweighted to turn into coarse pitch, but oil entering the hub under pressure (through a pipe running up the axis of the propeller) forces a central cylinder outwards, and cranks attached to the cylinder move the blades towards fine pitch. A constant speed unit varies the oil pressure automatically depending on engine speed, so that in theory the pilot does not need to adjust pitch manually, the CSU adjusting it automatically depending on throttle setting and allowing the engine to run at its most efficient speed. The counterweight is attached to the blades via a bracket; hence

BELOW A de Havilland hydromatic propeller. **Hydraulic pressure through the centre moves the piston fore-and-aft, moving the rotating cam that turns the blades via bevel gears.** (*Crown Copyright*)

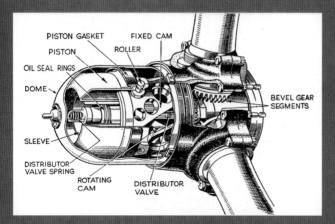

these are sometimes referred to as 'bracket-type' propellers. Spinners, which hide the counterweight mechanism, are usually fitted. This type is fitted to Pegasus-engined aircraft.

When the control lever is moved to the minimum rpm position, the blades are locked in fully coarse pitch, and the governor control becomes inoperative. These propellers cannot be feathered, but if the propeller of a failed engine is set this way, engine rpm may be reduced and drag is minimised.

Later Hydromatic propellers are controlled by oil pressure in both directions (rather than the counterweights), fore-and-aft movement of the piston causing a cam to turn that moves the blades via bevel gears. Early propellers have a 10°, 20° or 35° pitch range, later types have a 65° range and so can be feathered. This type is fitted to Mk II aircraft and to some Hercules-engined aircraft.

Rotol external cylinder propellers

These operate in a similar way to Hydromatic propellers, again with one piston being used to drive all the blades; this is mounted ahead of the hub, hence 'external' to distinguish it from early versions that have the cylinder inside the hub. Again, later versions can be feathered. Rotol R8 external cylinder propellers are fitted to some Hercules-engined aircraft.

Electric propellers

A reversible electric motor is mounted in front of the hub and has a 'no voltage' brake to prevent it turning unless powered. Current is picked up from four brushes and slip rings on the propeller shaft, the connections being feathering, fine pitch, coarse pitch, and a ground.

Control is by an electric governor unit – rather than oil pressure being applied to the propeller directly, it controls a piston in this unit that operates a jogging contact to cause current to flow one way or other to the motor. The feathering control, operated directly by a switch in the cockpit, applies a larger current to effect the feathering as quickly as possible.

Epicyclic gearing connects the motor to the blade hubs, but the high gear ratio required (around 1,000:1) means that operation is slow. The slip rings and brushes are also prone to wear and contamination, so need regular servicing. Curtiss electric propellers are fitted to Mk IV aircraft with Twin Wasps. Most Hercules-engined Wellingtons use Rotol RE9 or RE11 electric propellers.

Blades

Pegasus-engined Wellingtons use non-feathering de Havilland 20° 'bracket' propellers with aluminium blades.

Other Wellington propeller blades are usually wooden, some using Rotol's Jablo compressed wood and others from the Airscrew Company at Weybridge – the latter are lighter, an R8/36/2 weighing 390lb compared to a Jablo R8/36/1 at 455lb.

Bristol Hercules

Roy Fedden's main passion was for the sleeve-valve engine. This dispensed with conventional cylinder-head poppet valves by inserting an alloy steel sleeve between the piston and the cylinder wall; this was both rotated and moved up and down (in sync with engine rotation) by a train of gears from the crankshaft, and four carefully shaped ports in the sleeve allowed the combustion chamber to connect with the incoming fuel flow and exhaust pipe via five ports in the cylinder at the appropriate times in the stroke cycle. The sleeve-valve configuration offered the potential for greater power output and higher rotational speeds than conventional designs (because of timing issues with the conventional valves), and with no external valves, it was also slightly more compact. Although the lack of poppet valves meant that fewer parts were required, special alloys had to be used to prevent excessive wearing of the sleeve, and the sleeve-valve engine was more complicated to manufacture. The sleeves originally had to be precisely machined to fit both cylinder and piston, and machining of cylinders, sleeves, and pistons was done together to produce matched sets – this meant that pistons and sleeves were not easily interchangeable, which was a problem for the maintenance crews. This was not practical for mass production, and it was a development nightmare to resolve the problem, which delayed the introduction of this type of engine, but once in production it

was successfully produced in large numbers – around 65,000 Bristol Hercules were built, more than double the output of the Pegasus. Bristols remained the champion of the sleeve-valve engine, with no other manufacturers producing them in such large quantities – most were again built by shadow factories, including purpose-built premises at Accrington; this made about 15,000, with 40,000 coming from the car factories, and the remainder from Bristol's. The engines themselves also had longer service lives than in-line engines such as the Merlin.

Construction and overall layout of the Hercules was broadly similar to the Pegasus, the main differences being:

■ The sleeve-valve operating mechanism replaces the cam and tappet mechanism on the front face of the crankcase.
■ Addition of an internal divider in the crankcase between the two rows of cylinders.
■ Cylinders are made from aluminium alloy drop-forgings.
■ Cylinder heads are constructed with top and bottom parts (to overcome difficulties in machining the cooling fins), although after fitting they can be treated as one part.
■ The lower air intake is for the oil cooler, the carburettor air intake being mounted above the engine.

Hercules-engined Wellingtons are fitted with Hydromatic or electric variable-pitch propellers.

The Mk X and later marks typically use the Hercules VI or later XVI. These engines

BELOW Front (left) and rear (right) of the Hercules. The absence of cylinder head valve equipment is evident. *(Crown Copyright via The National Archives)*

RIGHT The sleeve-valve mechanism of the Hercules. (Crown Copyright via the National Archives)

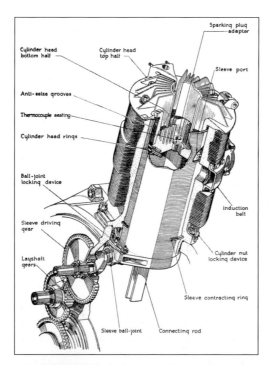

Sparking plug adaptor
Cylinder head top half
Cylinder head bottom half
Sleeve port
Anti-seize grooves
Thermocouple seating
Cylinder head rings
Induction belt
Ball-joint locking device
Sleeve driving gear
Cylinder nut locking device
Layshaft gears
Sleeve contracting ring
Sleeve ball-joint
Connecting rod

FAR RIGHT The sleeve can be seen in this view. The light grey cable is for operating the electric propeller. (Author)

RIGHT This Hercules at Brooklands has been sectioned. The lower cylinders are connected to the exhaust collector ring. (Author)

BELOW The Hercules exhaust system with flame damper and connections for cabin heating. (Crown Copyright)

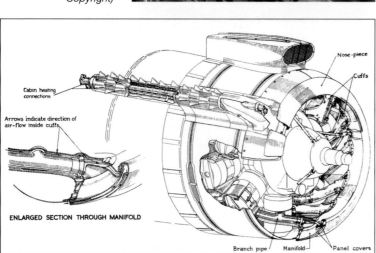

Cabin heating connections
Nose-piece
Cuffs
Arrows indicate direction of air-flow inside cuffs
ENLARGED SECTION THROUGH MANIFOLD
Branch pipe   Manifold   Panel covers

differ only in the carburettor, the latter having an automatic mixture control which interlinks the throttle to give a rich mixture at take-off and high power settings, but a weak mixture throughout the cruise regime for maximum fuel economy. This proved to be a challenge for Bristols, but the Air Ministry pressed for it as it could extend the range of the aircraft by up to 10% compared to manual mixture control. The Hercules XVII is a XVI modified for use by Coastal Command by locking the supercharger in low gear and reducing the impeller size to give increased power at low level.

The Mk V high-altitude Wellington was trialled with Hercules XI engines fitted with a turbocharger which uses the exhaust flow (energy which is otherwise wasted) to drive an impeller for extra boost, but the arrangement is technically complex and only efficient at high altitudes where the pressure differential is greatest.

The Hercules was popular with pilots, giving a smoother ride than the Pegasus and, with more power available, the aircraft had much better single-engine performance. The time between overhauls for all Wellington engines was around 400 hours. After the war, the Hercules TBO was gradually increased to over 3,500 hours.

One French Noratlas is still flying with Hercules engines, and there are other examples of ground-run demonstrators.

MAIN PARTICULARS – BRISTOL HERCULES VI

Type	Double-row, 14-cylinder, sleeve-valve, air-cooled radial	pressure	DTD672/80psi at 70°C at 2,000rpm
Firing order	1, 10, 5, 14, 9, 4, 13, 8, 3, 12, 7, 2, 11, 6 (cylinders are equally spaced and numbered 1–14 clockwise starting from the top, looking from the front; even-numbered cylinders are in the front row)	Carburettor	Claudel Hobson AIT 132M or MC
		Fuel pump pressure	9–10psi
		Carburettor fuel pressure	2.5psi
		Magnetos	Rotax NST 14/1, or BTH C2SE 14/S, or Simms FST 14S/1, or Simms FST 14S/3 (two fitted)
Bore/stroke	5.75in/6.5in		
Swept volume	2,366cu in (38.7 litres)	Spark plugs	Lodge type RS4R, or AC Sphinx type RZ4R
Compression ratio	7:1		
Supercharger gear ratio	6.68:1 (low gear 'M')/8.35:1 (high gear 'S')	Starter	Rotax 1231C electric (with hand-turning equipment)
Continuous power	1,400bhp at 2,400rpm	Propeller	Left-hand tractor Rotol electric variable-pitch, constant speed and feathering control, or de Havilland 35° variable-pitch, constant speed with or without feathering control, diameter 12ft 6in
Propeller reduction gear	Bevel epicyclic 0.444:1		
Diameter/length	52in/67.5in		
Weight (dry)	1,890lb		
Rated altitude	6,000ft ('M' gear)/15,000ft ('S' gear)		
Fuel type	DED2475 (100 octane)	Air Publication AP1728 gives full details of the installation, maintenance, and operation of the Hercules.	
Oil type/normal			

1 Constant-speed governor unit
2 Reduction-gear bevel pinion
3 Drive to rear sleeve
4 Propeller shaft
5 Stationary gear and front bevel gear
6 Rear bevel gear, thrust ring and reduction-gear driving wheel
7 Reduction-gear casing
8 Breather pipe
9 Front-cover drain pump
10 Drive to front sleeve
11 Sleeve
12 Piston
13 Sleeve crank
14 Articulated rod
15 Sleeve ball joint
16 Maneton joint
17 Front crankweb
18 Master rod
19 Crankshaft centre section and centre main bearing
20 Crankcase front chamber
21 Lifting sling guides
22 Cylinder
23 Cylinder head
24 Ignition harness
25 Engine mounting ring
26 Volute casing
27 Salomon dampers
28 Rear crankweb
29 Impeller
30 Impeller shaft
31 Impeller gear and centrifugal clutch
32 Spring drive gear
33 Two-speed clutch housing
34 Two-speed clutch
35 Connecting-rod oil-transfer plunger
36 Supercharger casing and diffuser vanes
37 Centrifuge
38 Crankcase rear chamber

39 Sump and no8 induction pipe
40 Sump filter
41 Induction pie drain-valve
42 Induction branch pipe
43 Oil feed to sleeve driving mechanism
44 Oil feed to two-speed clutches
45 Oil drain from volute casing and rear cover
46 Air intake

47 Carburettor
48 Scavenge return to carburettor
49 Magneto
50 Engine controls
51 Oil pump
52 Scavenge relief valve
53 Scavenge return from pump
54 Starter

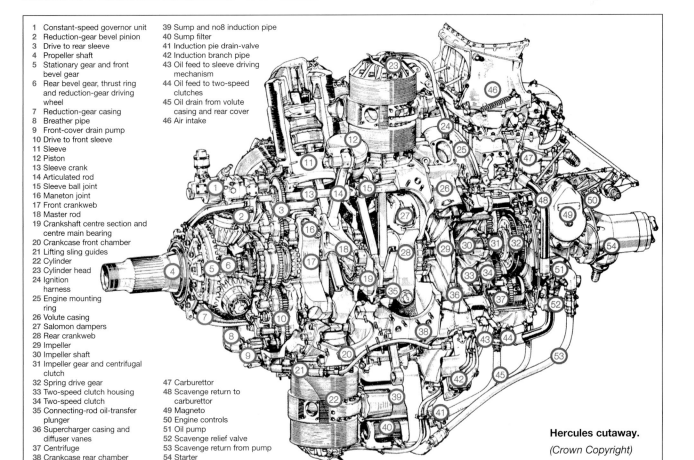

Hercules cutaway.

(Crown Copyright)

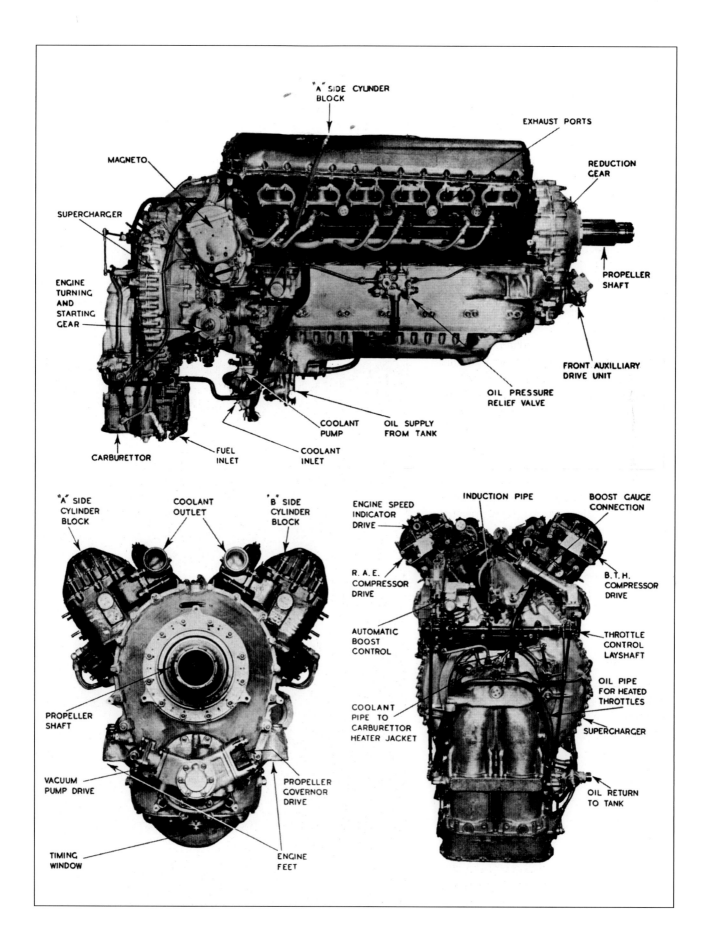

"A" SIDE CYLINDER BLOCK

EXHAUST PORTS

MAGNETO

REDUCTION GEAR

SUPERCHARGER

ENGINE TURNING AND STARTING GEAR

PROPELLER SHAFT

FRONT AUXILLIARY DRIVE UNIT

OIL PRESSURE RELIEF VALVE

COOLANT PUMP

OIL SUPPLY FROM TANK

CARBURETTOR

FUEL INLET

COOLANT INLET

"A" SIDE CYLINDER BLOCK

COOLANT OUTLET

"B" SIDE CYLINDER BLOCK

ENGINE SPEED INDICATOR DRIVE

INDUCTION PIPE

BOOST GAUGE CONNECTION

R. A. E. COMPRESSOR DRIVE

B.T.H. COMPRESSOR DRIVE

AUTOMATIC BOOST CONTROL

THROTTLE CONTROL LAYSHAFT

PROPELLER SHAFT

OIL PIPE FOR HEATED THROTTLES

COOLANT PIPE TO CARBURETTOR HEATER JACKET

SUPERCHARGER

VACUUM PUMP DRIVE

PROPELLER GOVERNOR DRIVE

OIL RETURN TO TANK

TIMING WINDOW

ENGINE FEET

Rolls-Royce Merlin

Having equipped the Wellington with 'power eggs' to facilitate the fitting of different engines, the first to be tried in place of the Pegasus was the Rolls-Royce Merlin X, this combination being designated the Wellington Mk II. Although the Merlin was more powerful than the Pegasus, it was also heavier, resulting in a forward movement of the aircraft centre of gravity, requiring additional tail ballast to be added and the main wheels to be moved forward 3in by extending the backstays. Despite these changes, the aircraft was found to have questionable pitch stability in the air. Trials with larger horn balances on the elevators were inconclusive, the issue finally being resolved by increasing the chord of the tailplane by extending the leading edge forward by 1ft (this modification was retained on later aircraft).

Although performance of the Wellington with the Merlin was satisfactory, priority for these engines was initially given to fighter aircraft, and later to the new front-line bombers (the Lancaster, Halifax, and Mosquito), so only 402 Mk IIs were built. Although the more powerful Merlin 60 was used on the high-altitude Mk VI aircraft, these did not see significant operational service.

Construction

The Merlin is a liquid-cooled V12 engine arranged as two parallel blocks of six cylinders with 60° between the blocks. A single aluminium casting forms the six cylinder heads for each block and carries valve ports and the coolant jacket, with four valve seats of silicon-chromium steel screwed into the top of each cylinder; 14 long studs hold each head to the crankcase. The pistons are machined from aluminium alloy forgings and have three gas rings and two scraper rings, and run in high-carbon steel liners.

A one-piece hollow six-throw crankshaft passes through the crankcase carried in seven bearings. The front of the crankshaft has a pinion driving a larger gear attached to the propeller, this combination acting as a 42% reduction gear. The nickel steel propeller shaft is carried in two roller bearings, the thrust being taken by a thrust ball bearing just behind the front roller bearing. The rear of the crankshaft transmits power to the overhead camshafts, two-speed supercharger, and other auxiliaries. Mixture is supplied by an SU carburettor. An air-cooled radiator is mounted beneath the forward part of the engine.

Merlin engines are still flying in many vintage aircraft, including Spitfires, Hurricanes, and Lancasters.

OPPOSITE 3-view of Merlin engine. This was the only in-line engine fitted to Wellingtons (Mk II and Mk VI). *(Crown Copyright)*

MAIN PARTICULARS – ROLLS-ROYCE MERLIN X

Type	12-cylinder, liquid-cooled 'V'
Firing order	1A, 6B, 4A, 3B, 2A, 5B, 6A, 1B, 3A, 4B, 5A, 2B (the starboard block is called 'A' and the port block 'B', with cylinders in each block being numbered from the propeller end)
Bore/stroke	5.4in/6in
Swept volume	1,647cu in (27 litres)
Compression ratio	6:1
Supercharger gear ratio	8.15:1 (low gear 'M')/9.49:1 (high gear 'S')
Continuous power	1,145bhp at 2,600rpm
Propeller reduction gear	Pinion and spur 0.42:1
Length/width/height	71in/29.8in/43in
Weight (dry)	1,640lb
Rated altitude	10,000ft ('M' gear)/18,000ft ('S' gear)
Fuel type/consumption	DED2475 (100 octane)/115 gal/hr, or DTD230 (87 octane)/94 gal/hr
Carburettor	Rolls-Royce, or SU AVT32, automatic mixture control
Fuel pump pressure	2–2¾psi
Magnetos	BTH C1SE 12S (two fitted)
Starter	Electric
Coolant	70% water/30% ethylene glycol to DTD344A
Propeller	Right-hand tractor de Havilland 35° variable-pitch, constant speed with or without feathering control, diameter 12ft 9in

Air Publication AP1590 gives full details of the installation, maintenance, and operation of the Merlin. For further information on this engine, see the Haynes Manuals for the Spitfire, Hurricane, and Lancaster.

ABOVE R1220 was the Mk IV prototype with Twin Wasp engines. *(Crown Copyright via Brooklands Museum)*

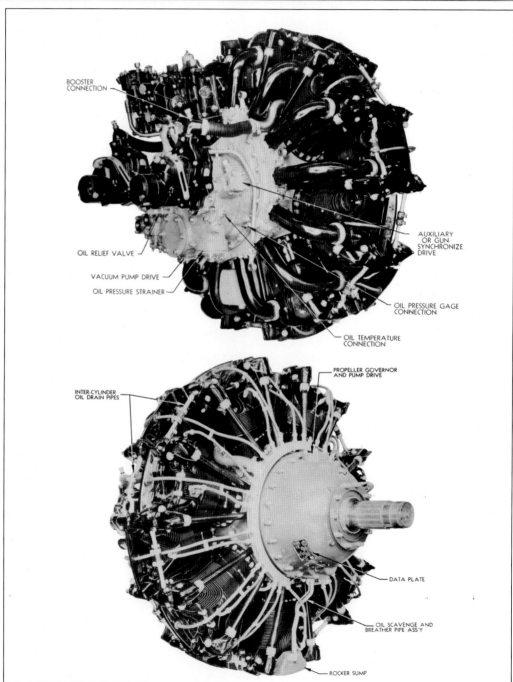

BOOSTER CONNECTION

AUXILIARY OR GUN SYNCHRONIZE DRIVE

OIL RELIEF VALVE

VACUUM PUMP DRIVE

OIL PRESSURE STRAINER

OIL PRESSURE GAGE CONNECTION

OIL TEMPERATURE CONNECTION

INTER-CYLINDER OIL DRAIN PIPES

PROPELLER GOVERNOR AND PUMP DRIVE

DATA PLATE

OIL SCAVENGE AND BREATHER PIPE ASS'Y

ROCKER SUMP

RIGHT Rear (top) and front (bottom) of the Twin Wasp. It is similar to a Hercules but with conventional valves. *(Crown Copyright via The National Archives)*

Pratt & Whitney Twin Wasp

Consideration had been given to using American engines on the Wellington from September 1939, but following some vacillation by the Air Ministry, the decision to proceed was not finalised until July 1940. Pratt & Whitney R-1830 S3C4-G Twin Wasps were made available; at least some of these having been destined for French aircraft, but the German invasion blocked their delivery. As this engine was similar in size and power to the Hercules (though with conventional valve gear), the task was completed quickly, the first aircraft flying in early December, and a total of 220 aircraft were built at the Broughton factory as the Mk IV. As the maintenance requirements were slightly different because of the American-specification parts, the aircraft tended not to be mixed with other marks on operational service, serving with only four bomber squadrons, and being used for night photography experiments with 544 Squadron.

General engine construction and layout is similar to the Pegasus, but with a divided crankcase for the two rows of cylinders, only two valves (one inlet and exhaust) per cylinder, and the supercharger has only one speed setting. Note that, although the Twin Wasp has a higher swept volume than the Hercules and has higher fuel consumption, it is only about 90% as powerful.

The Twin Wasp is particularly prone to the bottom cylinders filling with oil, and the engine must be hand turned before starting to check for hydraulic lock (and drained if found). The injection carburettor also means that, if the engine does not start immediately, it is likely to flood and also require draining.

Twin Wasp engines are still flying in many vintage aircraft, including DC-3 Dakotas and PBY-5A Catalinas.

Summary

Nearly 3,500 Wellingtons were powered by Pegasus engines, and the 7,328 aircraft powered by Hercules engines make up more than two-thirds of the total. With fewer than 500 aircraft using Merlins and 220 with the Twin Wasp, only 6% of Wellingtons used non-Bristol engines.

MAIN PARTICULARS – PRATT & WHITNEY TWIN WASP R-1830

Type	Double-row, 14-cylinder, poppet-valve, air-cooled radial (two valves per cylinder; cylinders are equally spaced and numbered 1–14 anti-clockwise starting from the top, looking from the front; even-numbered cylinders are in the front row)
Bore/stroke	5.5in/5.5in
Swept volume	1,830cu in (30 litres)
Compression ratio	6.7:1
Supercharger gear ratio	7.15:1
Continuous power	1,050bhp at 2,550rpm at 15,500ft with 5lb boost
Propeller reduction gear	Spur planetary 0.5:1
Diameter/length	48.2in/61.2in
Weight (dry)	1,463lb
Fuel type	RDE/F/100 (100 octane)
Oil type/normal pressure	DTD109/80psi at 60°C at 2,000rpm
Carburettor	PD-12BS, or PD-12H1, Stromberg injection carburettor with automatic mixture control
Fuel pump pressure	15psi
Magnetos	Scintilla SF14L-3, or Bosch magnetos (two fitted)
Propeller	Right-hand tractor Curtiss electric variable-pitch, constant speed and feathering control, diameter 12ft 3in

Air Publication AP1847 gives full details of the installation, maintenance, and operation of the Twin Wasp. For further information on this engine, see the Haynes Manual for the DC-3 Dakota.

Ivan Berryman

Chapter Five

The Loch Ness Wellington

The only preserved Wellington which saw active service is now on display at Brooklands Museum. This aircraft ditched in Loch Ness in 1940 and the wreck was discovered by chance. Raised from the loch in a dramatic recovery operation, 'R for Robert' has been painstakingly restored and now takes pride of place at the museum.

OPPOSITE 'R for Robert' flies over Brooklands, with the Vickers factory on the edge of the racing circuit. *(Painting by Ivan Berryman, reproduced by courtesy of Cranston Fine Arts)*

Introduction

In a hangar at Brooklands Museum in Surrey stands Wellington N2980 – known as 'R for Robert'. The story of the aircraft's journey back to Weybridge is a remarkable one, featuring luck (both good and bad), ingenuity, and hard work in large quantities. The aircraft now stands as a magnificent tribute to the men who built, flew, recovered, and restored it.

WHY IS 'R FOR ROBERT' A HISTORIC AIRCRAFT?

Of the two complete surviving Wellingtons, N2980 is the only one that actually saw operational service, but it is also a historic aircraft in its own right for several reasons:

- It took part in the Battle of Heligoland Bight on 18 December 1939, the raid being led by Wg Cdr Richard Kellett (who had led the record-breaking Wellesley flight from Ismailia to Darwin). It was largely the losses incurred on this raid that persuaded Bomber Command to abandon its reliance on daylight raids and switch to night bombing.
- The pilot of 'R for Robert' on this raid was Sqn Ldr Paul Harris, who had led Britain into battle on 4 September 1939 flying a Wellington during a raid on Brunsbüttel, the western entrance to the Kiel Canal.
- The bomber force, including 'R for Robert', heading to Heligoland on 3 December 1939 was detected by a radar station on the German island of Wangerooge – this is believed to be the first time an enemy bombing raid had been detected by radar.
- 'R for Robert' survived 14 raids over Germany, when the expected life of a Wellington was just six raids.
- The aircraft was flown by Vickers' Chief Test Pilot 'Mutt' Summers, on 16 November 1939.
- Archie Frazer-Nash and his partner Captain Thomson personally tested their Frazer-Nash gun turrets in this aircraft.
- The pilot of 'R for Robert' on its final flight was Sqn Ldr N.W. David Marwood-Elton, who later became an RAF intelligence officer whose duties included investigating targets for Barnes Wallis's 'bouncing bombs'. On 22 March 1944, while station commander at RAF Burn in Yorkshire, he went on a 'trip' to Frankfurt aboard a 578 Squadron Halifax LK-R (also 'R for Robert'); the aircraft was shot down, and the crew all spent the rest of the war as PoWs.

History

N2980 was approximately the 80th Mk IA to roll off the Weybridge production line, making its maiden flight in the hands of 'Mutt' Summers. It was taken on charge by 149 (East India) Squadron at RAF Mildenhall on 20 November 1939, being given the squadron code letter 'R'. No 149 was one of ten squadrons to be equipped with Wellingtons at this time. They had converted to the type at the start of the year and had already flown it on several operations, including the first RAF bombing raid of the war.

On 3 December, 24 Wellingtons were sent to bomb warships in the vicinity of Heligoland, two small islands that guard the approaches to the German North Sea ports. Half the force came from 149 Squadron, and the raid was led by Wg Cdr Richard Kellett, who had claimed the flight distance record with the LRDU Wellesleys the year before. The third of the four sections was led by Flt Lt Stewart flying N2980 on its first operational sortie. Two cruisers and other ships were spotted and bombed, with no apparent result, although the Germans recorded a minesweeper as sunk. The formations were attacked by Messerschmitt Bf 109 fighters, and one was shot down for no RAF losses. This luck was not to last. One Wellington had a bomb 'hang up', but this later fell away, hitting a gun emplacement on Heligoland – the first bomb of the war to fall on German soil.

A similar raid was mounted on 14 December, 99 Squadron sending out 12 Wellingtons to 'finish off' two damaged cruisers heading for Wilhelmshaven on the German coast. Low cloud kept the formation low, but it was located by German radar and Bf 109s and 110s intercepted it, shooting down three Wellingtons and, in the confusion, two more collided and went down into the sea. A further aircraft was damaged and crash-landed on returning to its base, killing three of the crew. One fighter was shot down, but at the cost of half of the attacking force. Remarkably, RAF officials attributed the losses to flak, unwilling to believe that a heavily armed bomber formation could be so badly mauled by fighter attack.

On 18 December, three squadrons (9, 37, and 149) sent out a total of 24 Wellingtons, including Sqn Ldr Paul Harris in N2980, to attack warships at Wilhelmshaven. The aircraft flew above 10,000ft and the weather was so clear that the German fighter pilots were not expecting any 'trade', but when radar picked up the bombers, they were quickly airborne. Thirty-eight fighters attacked, shooting down ten Wellingtons near the coast, with two ditching crossing the North Sea and three more written off after crash-landings. N2980 made it back safely, Harris and his second pilot both receiving DFCs. With fully half of the attacking force not returning, it was difficult for the 'top brass' to continue to think that 'the bomber will always get through', and this operation, which has come to be known as the 'Battle of Heligoland Bight', effectively marked the end of RAF daylight strategic bombing raids by large formations of aircraft.

'R for Robert' flew a further five operational sorties with 149 Squadron, including another attack on Heligoland and a 'nickel' operation to Hannover, as well as four training sweeps. With the Mk IA being the first Wellington equipped with three Frazer-Nash turrets, the company took a keen interest in the operational deployment of their equipment, and both Archie Frazer-Nash and his partner E.G. Thompson were regular visitors to Mildenhall during this period to fly in the aircraft – the gunners also learning much from the 'boffins'.

The aircraft was transferred to 37 Squadron at RAF Feltwell on 30 May 1940, and it flew a further seven bombing sorties to targets including the railway yards at Hamm, a synthetic oil plant at Mors, and München-Gladbach.

Having survived 14 operations at a time when just six missions was the average life expectancy of a Wellington, on 6 October 1940 the aircraft was taken on charge by 20 OTU at RAF Lossiemouth on the Moray Firth, one of the recently formed Operational Training Units for new crews. For this new duty, the aircraft was fitted with dual controls, another control column being installed in the second pilot's position, and the ventral turret was removed (although the ribs for supporting it remained). On the last afternoon of the year, Sqn Ldr Marwood-Elton, Plt Off Slatter, a wireless operator, a gunner, and four trainee navigators climbed aboard the aircraft and headed into the wintry

weather of the Great Glen. Flying at 8,000ft, the starboard engine cut out (it is believed that both magnetos had become faulty) and with mountains all around, the pilot ordered the crew to bale out. As the aircraft lost height, he spotted an expanse of water through the clouds and decided to ditch, which they did successfully with the port engine still running. Exiting the aircraft via the overhead hatches, the two pilots climbed into the emergency dinghy on the starboard side and paddled to the shore (which was only about 200yd away) looking back to see the Wellington sinking into the loch. They were picked up by a lorry on the shore road, and were back at Lossiemouth in time to take part in the New Year festivities. Later it was found that Sgt Fensome, the rear gunner, had pulled his ripcord too soon and his parachute had snagged and torn on the aircraft as he exited; he did not survive.

Location

The waters of Loch Ness attract many visitors each year on the lookout for 'Nessie', the loch's famous monster. During the late 1960s and into the '70s, ever more sophisticated apparatus was brought into the hunt, with aerial survey flights (including some performed by ex-Wellington pilot Ken Wallis in his autogyro) and underwater sonar scans. One such scan in 1976 located an aircraft wreck about a mile from the Bona Lighthouse, which marks where the loch ends and the River Ness begins. The aircraft was taken to be the wreck of a Catalina flying boat, and a team from the Underwater Technology group at Heriot-Watt University in Edinburgh thought that this would be an ideal target to demonstrate the underwater surveying apparatus that they had been developing. In the summer of 1978, one of their Remotely Operated Vehicles (ROV) located the wreck at a depth of 230ft, but the TV pictures fed up to the surface showed that the aircraft was in fact a Wellington – and in remarkably complete condition. Researches at the MoD suggested that this was likely to be N2980, and in 1979 the identity was confirmed by divers from the Royal Navy Deep Diving team from Portsmouth who were tasked with searching the wreck – only specialist divers

could reach this depth, which was far too deep for conventional scuba-divers.

The Heriot-Watt team, led by Robin Holmes, returned in 1980 to survey the site with their latest ROV, but they had only a brief glimpse of the wreck before bad weather curtailed the search. The ROV development project ended in early 1981, but funds were obtained to conduct another search later in the year and an extensive photo and video survey was carried out. This showed that the aircraft was no longer in such good condition, with the top of the fuselage (including the leading edge frame and

both upper longerons) torn open, presumably by souvenir hunters trawling clumsily for parts of the aircraft.

Recovery

Once identified as a rare and historic aircraft, there arose the possibility of recovering the aircraft. Over the next three years, Robin Holmes managed to interest a number of organisations in the project, and with their help – and funds – secured (or at least promised), the operation gathered pace. The key stage in the process was the creation in July 1984 of the Loch Ness Wellington Association Ltd as a charity, to which ownership of the wreck was formally transferred. This opened up additional sources of funding.

Prior to the 1981 survey, it had been thought possible to effect a recovery of the aircraft using the ROVs by remotely attaching cables to the main spar and tail, to which divers could then attach buoyancy bags to raise the aircraft near to the surface. It could then be towed to shallow water and lifted out by crane. As this needed only the services of the existing ROVs and scuba-divers, costs would be kept to a minimum. However, the damaged fuselage made such a plan unfeasible – it would have to be strengthened in some way. Fortunately, discussions with British Aerospace at Weybridge had brought Robin into contact with the Vintage Aircraft and Flying Association (VAFA) and its Chairman, Norman 'Spud' Boorer, who had worked on the design of the Wellington. 'Spud' agreed to design a lifting frame for the aircraft, and this was duly constructed and tested by BAe at Weybridge. Contacts at Weybridge had also mentioned the existence of a new museum at the Brooklands paddock site, adjacent to the BAe factory, and discussions with Morag Barton, the museum's founder and coordinator, led to the new museum being chosen as the home for the recovered aircraft.

The new salvage plan required the services of divers capable of working on the wreck itself, and although the Royal Navy divers were using it for practice dives, they could not be expected to participate in a commercial recovery (though they did perform some useful 'housekeeping' duties on the site, such as

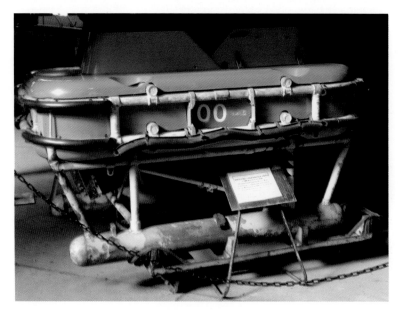

recovery of some small parts of the aircraft, including some geodetics which were tested for strength by BAe and found to be in excellent condition). The logical alternative was to employ divers from the North Sea oilfields – but with costs upwards of £10,000 per day and the recovery operation expected to take at least seven days, the budget could not stretch to that. However, the available funds and Robin's sweet-talking skills had managed to secure the services of Oceaneering International Services Ltd and their Atmospheric Diving Suit (ADS) – a hard articulated shell that allowed a man to work at depth for extended periods. The BBC expressed an interest in recording the recovery for a series on underwater archaeology.

The operation was scheduled, and by Tuesday 10 September 1985, the lifting frame had been assembled onshore and the former Kessock ferry *Eilean Dubh* was anchored over the wreck site with two ADSs (called WASP and JIM) secured aboard. Next day, WASP was lowered to the bottom, but the positioning had been inaccurate, and by the time the *Eilean Dubh* had been moved directly above the wreck, the day was over. Before the frame could be sent down, a strengthening beam had to be inserted along the top of the fuselage to replace the damaged geodetics and take the weight of the tail. This proved awkward until an obstruction was pulled clear – it turned out to be the rudder – and this took most of the next day. The operation was now two days behind schedule, and this stretched to four, as the weather was too rough to work on Friday and Saturday. Sunday was better, but more time was lost repositioning the *Eilean Dubh*, which had moved in the stormy weather, and even more as WASP had to cut away a fishing net which was found to have draped itself over the forward fuselage since the wreck had been surveyed. The lifting straps could then be attached to the wreck, but Sunday also meant time was up for WASP. Fortunately Oceaneering were able to extend their commitment and remain on site.

The weather continued to improve and in the early hours of Monday, the barge with the lifting frame was towed out to the site. It was connected to the small crane on the *Eilean Dubh* and the buoyancy bags deflated to allow

it to sink over the wreck. Both ADSs worked to secure the 11 lifting straps between the wreck and the frame, but by dawn, with only six straps attached, the two divers had been working for 18 hours and were exhausted, so they had to rest. Meanwhile, numerous VIPs had been arriving at the operations base at the nearby Clansman Hotel, including David Marwood-Elton and Paul Harris, who had been invited to witness the recovery of 'their' aircraft. A dinner had been planned for that evening to celebrate a successful operation, but although the aircraft was still on the bottom, the dinner went ahead in a mood of cautious optimism. The press and public had also been out in force during the operation, vying for the best spots to catch the first glimpse of the 'monster' coming out of the loch.

The final connections were made on Tuesday afternoon, and WASP was recovered.

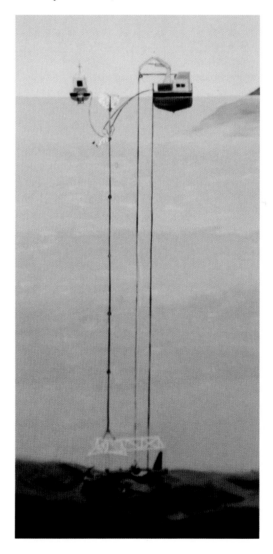

LEFT Scale illustration of the recovery process, showing (on the bottom) 'R for Robert', the original lifting frame and ADS (Atmospheric Diving Suit), and (on the surface) the workboats and buoyancy bags. *(Brooklands Museum)*

Compressed air was slowly pumped into the two buoyancy bags, building to an upward force of five tonnes each. Suddenly, the bags surfaced, and bobbed high on the calm loch – but all was not calm beneath, as when the cable was winched in, it brought to the surface only a tangle of aluminium. The frame had collapsed, and with it the confident mood. It appeared to be 'game over', but the press coverage had generated such interest from the public and businesses that money was suddenly flowing in and this was enough to continue funding the recovery – if the operation was still possible. On Wednesday, WASP was sent down to inspect the wreck, and found that the strengthening beam had bent and the tail section had parted from the rest of the aircraft, but the wings and centre fuselage were intact and the lifting straps which had torn from the frame were still attached.

A revised scheme to lift the main section was quickly drawn up, as was a new lifting frame, and plans for the latter were rushed to nearby Cromarty Firth Engineering Ltd to make it up – which they did in record time, delivering it to the site on the Thursday afternoon with the white paint still wet. By the end of the day, the frame was assembled and WASP had made the wreck ready for it. The frame-lowering operation was repeated on the Friday, and by evening it was attached and ready for the lift. The buoyancy bags were gently filled again, but when they surfaced this time, there was

a difference – they floated low in the water, indicating that they were carrying a substantial weight – 'R for Robert' was free of the bottom. It was now just a case of attaching a new pair of bags ten metres down the cable and filling them, then repeating this process, and this proved so straightforward that by just after 2:00am on the morning of Saturday 21 September, the aircraft was just five metres below the surface. Divers confirmed that this was the case, and also that the nose turret had gone, probably torn free as the aircraft pivoted off the bottom. However, this discovery did little to dampen the spirits of the recovery team.

With the wreck suspended just out of sight, it had to be towed slowly to the shore – taking nearly six hours to travel just over a mile to the head of the loch, where it was grounded. To negotiate the shallow water at the recovery site, the buoyancy bags had to be re-rigged directly on to the main spar, and as they were inflated for the final time, a wingtip broke the surface to the delight of the huge crowd of spectators that had again gathered in expectation. Now just beneath the surface, the Wellington was towed round into the mouth of the River Ness where a mobile crane awaited to lift it on to a barge … but the river current caught it and two of the onlookers' cabin cruisers had to give chase and pull it back under the crane, where it was secured to the shore. The divers quickly attached a cable and, at 7:45pm, the aircraft was lifted clear of the water, accompanied by

BELOW The wingtip of 'R for Robert' breaks the surface at last. (BAE Systems via Robin Holmes)

BELOW RIGHT The wings and centre section are lifted clear of the water. (BAE Systems via Robin Holmes)

some groaning from the straining geodetics
and the unrestrained delight of both the crowd
and the recovery team. In the gathering gloom,
Robin Holmes noticed a strange irony – the
crane had been built in Wilhelmshaven, one of
'R for Robert's' targets 46 years earlier!

First on board the aircraft the following
morning were the RAF's Explosive Ordnance
Disposal (EOD) team, and some .303
ammunition and marker floats were found and
removed. Next in were the Fire Brigade, who
used their hoses to wash out the worst of the
silt before the VAFA team started their recovery
and preservation work. Meanwhile, WASP had
been busy again, and the tail section (including
the rear turret) had been recovered using the
same technique as the main section. This
was lifted out on to the shore by the crane
and, after the EOD experts had removed the
ammunition from the turret, the crowd gathered
round. In less than 48 hours, the VAFA team
had dismantled the main section into its
component parts, and these were rearranged
on the barge ready for transportation the short
distance through the Caledonian Canal to
Inverness on 25 September. The VAFA wizards
had managed to acquire a Queen Mary trailer,

the long low-loader used throughout the war
for the transport of damaged aircraft, and the
Wellington's centre fuselage and parts of the
wing were craned aboard, the other parts going
on to two more modern articulated lorries, and
the strange convoy set off for Weybridge.

'R for Robert' arrived at the Brooklands
clubhouse in the early evening of Friday
27 September, the welcoming committee

LEFT The crowd watch as 'R for Robert' is dismantled for transportation. *(Brooklands Museum)*

including Morag Barton, civil dignitaries from the local council, and many past and present employees of Vickers/British Aerospace.

In May 1987, a team including the Royal Navy Diving Group recovered the front turret from Loch Ness, and at the end of the year, a sub-aqua group from RAF Kinloss dived at the location where the wreck had first grounded, from where they recovered the remains of the pilot's seat, throttle box, flare chute, pitot head, and various other parts.

BELOW Detail of the smashed forward fuselage section. The nose turret had broken away and was recovered later. *(Brooklands Museum)*

ABOVE The tail with fin removed. Note the tail turret turned to the beam for the gunner's escape – sadly, he did not survive. *(Brooklands Museum)*

RIGHT Arriving at Brooklands Museum on a Queen Mary trailer, the fuselage and other parts of 'R for Robert' come home. *(Brooklands Museum)*

Restoration – structure

Once the excitement of the recovery had died down, a rather alarming fact became clear to the Brooklands staff – 'R for Robert' was in a terrible state, and even in wartime an aircraft in this condition would have been written off! In general, the structure that remained was in fairly good condition, but large sections of it were missing – most of the fuselage from the trailing edge to the tail, and from the cockpit forward to the front turret (which itself had not been recovered at this stage). Within the aircraft, the condition of fittings varied enormously, but it was clear that cleaning and preservation was required, including the arresting of corrosion throughout (even though Loch Ness is fresh water). All fittings were removed, with the intention of putting back as many as possible after refurbishment, including hydraulic, pneumatic, and electrical systems. In the event, insufficient information was kept on many small parts, so it became impossible to refit some of them later.

The museum had established a Wellington Preservation Policy Committee, which included Morag Barton, other museum staff, Hugh Tyrer, and Bob Casbard who was in charge of the restoration project, and this committee guided the project. One key decision that had to be taken right away was whether to display the aircraft as it had been found, or to attempt to return it wholly or partly to its factory condition. The RAF Museum displays Halifax W1048 (which had been recovered from a lake in Norway in 1973) in an unrestored condition, but the Brooklands team felt that N2980 had to be recognisable as a bomber, and presented complete and standing on its wheels, although there was no intention to return it to 'new' condition. In autumn 1986, the restoration decision was reversed briefly, but it was reinstated after further consideration. A policy was also declared of retaining as much of the original aircraft structure and fittings as

RIGHT **Before and after. With lots of ferrous metal, the rear turret is a bit of a mess after recovery, but it has been carefully restored.** (Brooklands Museum/Author)

ABOVE **Before and after. Inside the rear fuselage looking towards the turret just after recovery, and as it appears now.** (Brooklands Museum/Author)

BELOW **The nacelles and inner wings during restoration.** (Brooklands Museum)

possible to retain its authenticity, and clearly documenting which parts were not original. The hangar housing the aircraft would be open to the public throughout so that they could see the work as it progressed, latterly with a specially constructed viewing platform.

Central to being able to display the aircraft standing on its wheels was the strength of the structure. Although the wings and main spar were in good condition, the leading and trailing edge 'D' frames were badly corroded (the leading-edge frame was also split open at the top) and the top geodetic panel between these frames was virtually non-existent – there was no way this structure could support the weight of the aircraft. However, a solution presented itself from an unexpected source – three months after the recovery, the BBC aired its documentary, *One of Our Bombers is No Longer Missing*, about the recovery operation. The fuselage structure was recognised by a Lincolnshire gardener, who had been using the same thing as a greenhouse since it was purchased from a scrapyard in the 1950s. He contacted Brooklands Museum and agreed to donate his framework to the museum, the museum purchasing him a new greenhouse in exchange. By remarkable chance, it was exactly the section required, including the two 'D' frames, and was in good condition. The decision was thus made to replace the centre section of the aircraft with the 'greenhouse' structure, and use the aircraft section as the

basis of a separate 'walk through' exhibit to allow visitors to see the geodetic structure up close (as the aircraft itself would not be generally accessible by members of the public). Work on this exhibit proceeded in parallel with the work on the aircraft.

With the BAe Weybridge factory literally just across the road, the museum was fortunate in having a major local company with a strong interest in the restoration project, and also a large cluster of former employees – many of whom had worked on Wellingtons – whose services were now available as volunteers. A large number of documents were 'rescued' from the factory just before it closed in 1988, and were transferred to the Brooklands site. These included around 200 paper or linen Wellington drawings, plus thousands of microfilmed drawings, which were invaluable during the rebuild (although a complete set of detailed drawings of the aircraft does not exist, with many major assemblies missing from the microfilms).

Replacement geodetics were needed in large quantities, so British Alcan were asked for help and they produced around 1½ miles of geodetic section. It was extruded, rather than rolled from flat strip, which made it slightly thicker than the original, but this was not a major problem. With no machine to add curvature to the members, a process was developed whereby the members could be hammered to shape around a wooden block. Alcan also agreed to make the butterfly connectors on condition that Brooklands paid for the manufacture of the dies; and for this cost – just £850 – they acquired all of the aluminium structure required for the whole project (and some to spare). Additional sections of geodetics recovered from the loch were refitted, and some sections from other wrecks were also incorporated where possible, in preference for new material. Original geodetics were treated with dewatering fluid, and a corrosion-prevention fluid was also sprayed on to provide a thin protective film on the metal. Around 20,000 pop rivets were used during the rebuilding of the structure.

The first task in the fuselage rebuild was the installation of the 'greenhouse' top panel and the two 'D' frames, and this was complete by mid-1989. New longeron tubes were then added ahead of this section with the refurbished

BELOW The forward fuselage longerons are in place, and work has started on the replacement geodetics. *(Jonathan Falconer)*

12½ frame, allowing work to start on replacing the nose geodetics, a new 5½ frame being installed in autumn 1990, and the sides almost completed a year later. New longerons were also added aft to connect up the tail section, and work on the geodetics in that area continued in parallel with the nose. The whole fuselage, which had been sitting on the ground, had to be raised about 6ft in 1992 to facilitate work on the underside geodetics, which were largely complete by early 1993. The final tasks on the main fuselage, in spring 1994, were installation of the ventral turret fitting and the refurbished bomb beam and bomb doors.

The outer wings were refurbished by Royal Aeronautical Society volunteers at the Monarch Aircraft Engineering site at Luton throughout 1988–89. The starboard inner wing had suffered some damage during recovery and needed to be rebuilt, including the root rib, but both inner wings were refitted to the fuselage in early 1992. The main spar tubes were injected with lanolin to exclude air that might corrode them from the inside. Both engine nacelles were completely stripped and rebuilt, this being completed after first checking the fit on the inner wings, allowing the undercarriage and new undercarriage doors to be fitted in 1993. After the inner wings and one of the engines had been refitted, an ex-Vickers engineer was visiting the hangar and noticed that the spar box – a strut between the top and bottom of the main spar at the centreline joints – was missing! Museum staff

ABOVE **The partly rebuilt fuselage with the inner wing and engine.** *(Jonathan Falconer)*

were unsure where it was, but after a quick search round the hangar the visitor found it, and it was subsequently refitted.

Refurbishment and reattachment of the tail surfaces was straightforward compared to the other structural elements, although damage to the rudder meant that a new one was needed. This was fabricated by BAe Kingston incorporating some of the undamaged parts from the original rudder. All of the tail surfaces were in place by spring 1993.

Although the main restoration work took place in the 'Wellington Hangar', a 1940-built Bellman hangar in front of the Brooklands clubhouse, many of the volunteers were able to remove parts to work on in their own workshops and sheds at home. With up to 20 volunteers

LEFT **The starboard inner wing, showing the main spar, wing root rib structure, and reconstruction of the leading edge spar.** *(Jonathan Falconer)*

RIGHT The restored rear fuselage. Most of the structure seen here is new geodetics. *(Author)*

BELOW The structure forward of the cockpit is also mostly new geodetics. Note the 'one cell' window above the bomb aimer's compartment. *(Author)*

working on the aircraft each day, this relieved some congestion in the hanger. Some new parts (such as the second pilot's floor and rudder pedals) were built from scratch by volunteers in the museum, and by others working at home. These included the 5½ frame in the nose, which was missing completely from the wreck. Some machining and welding was also done by students at nearby Brooklands College.

The port engine was reinstalled on 28 April 1994 and the starboard on 11 May (although this may have been a temporary test fitting). A week later was a red-letter day for the restoration team, as the jacks were removed to lower the aircraft on to its main wheels (and tail wheel axle). It was to the team's great credit – and relief – that this was accomplished with scarcely a creak from the airframe.

The fuel tanks were installed in the outer wings (which had already been refitted with the ailerons and flaps), and these were reattached, with the wingtips being fitted in September 1994, marking completion of the principal work on the aircraft structure.

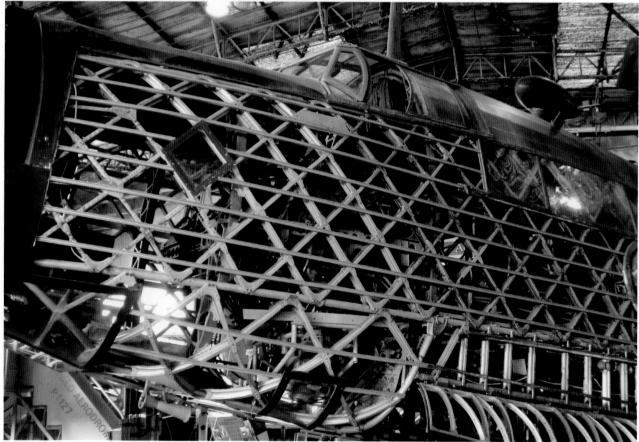

LEFT Work has begun on the fuselage. Note the Frise ailerons on the table – the leading edge protrusions reduce control forces. *(Jonathan Falconer)*

BELOW By 1990, the central fuselage was rebuilt and various subsections had been restored, but the fuselage ends are still to be reconstructed. *(Brooklands Museum)*

Restoration – other fixtures and fittings

Numerous external organisations were approached to assist with the restoration, and many agreed to refurbish parts of the aircraft. Preliminary restoration work on the turrets was undertaken by their original builders Frazer-Nash, although further work was required by the Brooklands team to bring these up to the desired standard, and they were refitted before the aircraft was stood back on its wheels. Despite the murky appearance of the Perspex on recovery, all of it was found to be still in place and it cleaned up extremely well.

Lord King, Chairman of British Airways, took a personal interest in the project and provided a workshop at Heathrow in which around 25 former BA employees were able to work on sections of the aircraft, notably the port engine, cooling gills (for both engines), both undercarriage mechanisms, 12½ frame, and the chassis for the pilot's seat and controls. The BA team also made a new underpan for the nose gun turret and restored the original for the rear turret. The starboard engine was refurbished by the Rolls-Royce Heritage Trust at Bristol, some of their volunteers having worked at Bristol building the original engines. Both engines were displayed at Brooklands during periods when refurbishment was not taking place.

The main wheels and tyres were sent to Dunlop for inspection, but they reported that the tyres were beyond repair and the alloy wheels

had almost totally disintegrated, with just the brake units remaining usable. Fortunately, a pair of wheels and tyres from a Viking were acquired. These were identical to those on later Wellingtons (the wheels were smaller than those on a Mk IA, but they had the same axle fittings). When the undercarriage structure was overhauled by the BA team at Heathrow, the requirement was that it be capable of supporting the weight of the aircraft (axle stands are used, so the tyres are not carrying the weight). The oleos were depressurised and filled up to make them solid. As the aircraft was rebuilt where it is now displayed, it has never rolled any distance on its new undercarriage, and the solid oleos mean that this would have to be done very gently.

In December 1993, Bob Casbard retired as Wellington Project Leader, although he remained involved in the restoration. He was succeeded by John Lattimore, who had recently retired from his job as the Chief Fleet Engineer of Concorde. His main challenge was coordination – although work was proceeding steadily, with shifts running six days a week, each shift was generally doing its own part of the job, making overall progress appear slower.

Once the main structure was largely complete, it was possible to work on the internal fitments. The cockpit area had been severely damaged and the instrument panel had to be renewed, but it is fully 'populated' with original instruments of the correct type sourced from around the UK. The pilot's controls are all original (though some parted from the aircraft during the recovery and had to be brought to the surface separately). Parts of the pilot's seat frame are new, but the seat pan and the leather cushions are original, the latter having been restored by specialists at Portsmouth Museum. Original cockpit canopies were obtained from Cardington and the RAF Museum, and these were incorporated into the aircraft and the 'walk through' exhibit.

All of the original fabric was beyond repair, and it was decided to only partly re-cover the aircraft – the top of the fuselage and the rear fuselage sides being covered to keep out the worst of the dust from the refurbished interior and to display the aircraft markings, while leaving the rest of the structure exposed to view. The fabric rails fitted to the fuselage are all of the 'locking' type for convenience; originally, intermediate rails were plain strips. The fabric was carefully attached by hand (in smaller sections than on original aircraft), being pinned with drawing pins until the joins were taped over (not sewn as on the original), after which the drawing pins were removed. The covering was doped with the same layers as the original aircraft (except for the white dope layer), and as coloured dope was no longer available, Humbrol model enamel was used for the topcoat. A few short lengths of the original fabric rails were in good enough condition to be refitted, and these are located in the uncovered section.

Originally, it had been intended to straighten the starboard propeller and leave the port propeller bent, but both propellers were left unstraightened (they had been turning at impact, but the port one was under power and so was bent more). They were stripped, cleaned, and repainted by BAe Air Weapons Division in Bolton.

A small section of the hydraulic system was brought back to working order (powered externally), allowing some of the bomb door sections to be opened and closed.

The main phase of reconstruction lasted about ten years, so that by the late 1990s the aircraft was largely complete as it can be seen today. However, the work has never stopped completely, and continues on the inside, some electrical panels having been recently refitted.

A job well done

Wellington 'R for Robert' now stands magnificently in the corner of the hangar where it was rebuilt, as the centrepiece of an exhibition relating to the aircraft built at Weybridge. Visitors to Brooklands looking at the aircraft might be forgiven for thinking 'It'll be nice when it's finished', but the appearance of the aircraft today can only be described as remarkable, considering its spell underwater, and the magnitude of the reconstruction job can only be truly appreciated by studying pictures of the aircraft's condition when it arrived at Brooklands. Around 250 people worked on the restoration during the first ten years of the project, and they recorded around 100,000 man hours of effort on the Wellington – all this by Brooklands volunteers alone, so it does not include some of the large refurbishment tasks undertaken elsewhere.

The museum stuck to its praiseworthy policy of refurbishing and refitting as much of the original aircraft as possible, using contemporary substitutes where available, and only falling back on new materials as a last resort. The result is a true and lasting tribute to the people who built, recovered, and restored the aircraft for the public to enjoy for the future.

BELOW A gathering of Wellington veterans marked the 75th anniversary of the B.9/32's first flight, including Ken Wallis (with beard), Robin Holmes (in pink jumper), and actress Penelope Keith (who is a trustee of Brooklands Museum). *(Author)*

Chapter Six

The Crews' View

The Wellington was well loved by the crews who flew in it, and it was generally considered to be a safe aircraft with few vices. It was spacious and comfortable for its time, with a good view from the cockpit. Emergency escape and ditching provision was the best available.

OPPOSITE The pilot's view. The 'lump' on the nose is the top pivot for the nose turret. N2980 shares the hangar with other historic aircraft, including a Vickers Vimy. *(Author)*

Introduction

The crew of a Wellington was originally five – pilot (captain), second pilot, observer (who performed duties of navigator and bomb aimer), and two gunners, one of whom would also operate the wireless. Typically the second pilot was newly qualified and flew a few operations to gain experience before being given his own command. Later, the observer category was formally renamed navigator, and the front gunner (who was largely redundant on night operations) would have been wireless operator (who often had little to do as there was radio silence most of the time). Wellington crews liked the aircraft, and were confident that it would get them home.

The pilot's view

After taking the B.9/32 prototype K4049 up for an uneventful maiden flight in June 1936, 'Mutt' Summers is quoted as saying, 'Don't touch a thing'; indicating that everything was fine as it was, and echoing a similar statement that he made following his first flight in the Spitfire three months earlier. K4049 was found to have excellent all-round performance, was aerodynamically stable and was self-righting. However, the production Mk I was found to be nose-heavy. This was traced to a change in the elevator from horn balance in the prototype to tabs, and experimentation was required to find a

solution, which included the interconnection of the flaps and elevators.

Early flight tests were conducted by Summers, Bob Handasyde, Maurice Hare, and Jeffrey Quill, sometimes with Wallis, Westbrook or other Vickers staff aboard. Later, they were joined by Alex Henshaw and Maurice Summers (brother of 'Mutt'). As well as the huge amount of production testing, flight-testing continued to try different configurations of engines, gills, carburettors, rudder, elevators, tailplane, trim tabs, propellers, cabin heating, and so on throughout the production life of the aircraft.

Service pilots who had flown the preceding generation of aircraft with open cockpits could find the Wellington's rather claustrophobic, but with its leather seat back and padding behind the knees, the cockpit was seen by others as 'luxury'. Some pilots (even experienced ones) found themselves operating retractable undercarriage for the first time.

Operationally, crews typically flew only one type of aircraft, making contemporary comparisons difficult. However, RAE test pilot Eric Brown flew many types, including the Wellington, Whitley, and Hampden. He found the 'ponderous' Whitley to be the slowest with 'generally poor performance compared to the others' especially on one engine. The Hampden had 'better performance than the Whitley except in the matter of service ceiling' but it had 'poor directional stability that in certain flight conditions could lead to dangerous rudder overbalance'. The Wellington had similar performance to the Hampden 'but its flying characteristics gave it the edge over the other two' and its 'outstanding feature was its ability to absorb battle damage'. He witnessed a Wellington making a safe landing at Farnborough with most of its fin and rudder missing and other damage to the horizontal stabiliser and elevators, having been hit by flak over Rotterdam over 200 miles away. Thus his 'inevitable conclusion from a pilot's viewpoint was that the Wellington was clearly the best operational aircraft of the three'.

Pilots describe the aircraft with flattering terms such as 'docile', 'friendly', 'forgiving', 'stable', 'good-natured', and 'viceless'. It had a good view from the cockpit, and it was regarded as easy to fly (often even in

BELOW The pilot's seat with cushioned knee supports. The lever like a car handbrake is for seat height adjustment. *(Author)*

comparison with single-engined aircraft). Minor quibbles were a tendency to swing to starboard on take-off and some 'twitching' in flight. The latter was because of the airframe's flexibility, and 'Mutt' Summers used to say in humorous exaggeration that if you looped it, the wingtips touched – and crews were certainly able to see the wings bending in flight. Ken Wallis (who recorded over 1,200 hours flying Wellingtons, and later achieved fame for his autogyros) was quite happy to do aerobatics in one when doing fighter affiliation exercises – so much so that he was ordered to 'tone it down'! However, like all large aircraft, deliberate spinning was inadvisable.

Only two features of the Wellington come in for sustained criticism – one was the single-engine performance of the Pegasus aircraft. Running at full power, the remaining engine would heat up and had to be throttled back, resulting in a loss of height at the rate of about 100ft/min until the aircraft encountered ground effect, and might just stagger home that way. The other was the heating system that, even when it was working, was never very good (perhaps not surprising in a fabric-covered aircraft). The hot-air system to the front crew positions was adequate by the start of the war, but the rear turret system was always unsatisfactory and the gunner had to wear an electrically heated suit (temperature was controlled only by unplugging the suit periodically). Sometimes the gunners did not realise how hot the suit was and got burnt. All aircrew wore thick clothing, but would often return with lumps of ice from their breath on the front of their suits. Conversely, for tropical service, aircrew had to be issued with chamois gloves, to protect them from hot metal parts. The position of the airscrews, almost in line with the pilot, also caused some concern, especially in icing conditions.

The Merlin delivered 25% more power, and the Hercules 50% more, than the Pegasus and, with feathering propellers too, these engines gave acceptable single-engine performance. The Merlin

RIGHT On the right-hand panel are the brake indicators, fire extinguisher buttons, and oxygen gauges. *(Author)*

ABOVE The main engine controls are grouped into a unit on the pilot's left-hand side. *(Author)*

LEFT The main flight instruments are grouped in the blind flying panel (left). The centre panel (below) has most of the engine instruments. *(Author)*

ABOVE The starboard side of the instrument panel has the brake pressure gauge, oxygen gauges, and buttons for the fire extinguishers. The grey box is a remote camera control. *(Author)*

RIGHT The second pilot's position, his seat folded down on the starboard side. The dual controls were fitted to this aircraft when it moved to OTU duties. *(Author)*

RIGHT The pilot's control column. The two handles behind the 'spectacles' grip are for the main wheel brakes. *(Author)*

was found to be noisier than the radial engines and changed the performance of the aircraft more than the Hercules, which was found to give 'control and general behaviour … similar in every respect to the standard Pegasus Wellington'.

The autopilot occasionally gave 'nasty surprises', disengaging without warning, so the pilot had to be ready quickly to take control.

Cockpit drill (Mk III/X, other marks similar)

Pre-flight checks

Before entering the aircraft, check for foreign objects on the ground near the propellers. Tyres should be checked for creep, cuts, and even pressure, with chocks in place. Oleo compression should be even, the pitot head cover should be removed, and the ground starter battery plugged in.

On entering the aircraft, proceed into the fuselage to check the tank cocks for the main, nacelle, and overload fuel tanks (if carried), and the suction balance cock (which switches fuel from one side of the aircraft to the other); main tank cocks should be on and all other cocks should be off.

Once seated, check all flying controls (ailerons, elevator, and rudder, including trimming tabs) for full and free movement. Note that trimming tabs for elevator and rudder operate in the 'natural sense', that is a forward movement of the star wheel gives a nose-down attitude, and turning the rudder bias control (mounted on the elevator trim control) clockwise causes the aircraft to turn to starboard (and vice versa). The aileron tab control, however, does not operate in the 'natural sense', being turned to the right to raise the starboard wing. Adjust the rudder bar as required.

Check the brakes (on), ignition switches (off), undercarriage selector (down, with safety catch engaged), and undercarriage emergency knob ('normal'). Switch on undercarriage and flap indicators, and check all lights are green. Test the warning horn. Check the flaps (fully up) and flap selector (neutral), landing lights control lever (up) and landing lights (up, verified by ground crew), and bomb door control (closed).

To start the engines, set master cocks (on) and apply safety catch. Check the balance cock (off), open throttles ¼in and set mixture controls (if manual) to 'normal', propeller speed controls fully forward (high rpm), supercharger control (medium), carburettor air intake control (cold), cowling gills (open), oil cooler shutters (closed – Mk III only). Groundcrew manually turn each propeller at least two complete revolutions (so that any oil which has drained into the lower cylinders does not cause a hydraulic lock of pistons or sleeves), then start to prime the induction system.

To start the first engine, switch on the ignition and press the starter and booster coil buttons, allowing the engine to turn for no more than 20 seconds. If it does not fire, wait 30 seconds between attempts. Groundcrew continue to prime as the engine turns over. The starter button should be released as soon as the engine fires, but the booster coil button should continue to be held. Engine priming will normally continue after the engine has fired, until it picks up on the carburettor, after which the priming pump should be screwed down, the priming cock turned off, and the cowling door closed. The booster coil button can be released when the engine is running satisfactorily. The engine can then be brought up to 1,200rpm (checking that the oil pressure does not rise above 140psi, otherwise the oil cooler may be damaged) and the engine warmed up at this speed. The second engine can then be started in the same fashion, and the ground starter battery disconnected. All hatches should then be closed before proceeding with engine tests. Fuel tank contents should be checked, and oil temperatures and pressures should be monitored during warming up to a cylinder temperature of 120°C, oil temperature 15°C, and pressure 75psi. Check that all magnetos are functioning.

Test the hydraulic system by lowering and raising the flaps, returning the flap control lever to neutral.

Open up to 1,500rpm, and check operation of the two-speed supercharger (oil pressure drops momentarily at each change of setting). One engine at a time, run up to maximum weak continuous boost in rich mixture and check operation of the constant speed propeller (rpm should fall to 1,600 with the control fully back).

After a repair or inspection (or at the pilot's discretion), further checks can be made. With the propeller controls fully forward, open the throttle fully and check the take-off boost and static rpm. Throttle back to maximum rich continuous boost plus 2½lb (or more if necessary) to ensure that the rpm begin to fall to below 2,800. Test each magneto in turn – the single ignition drop should not exceed 50rpm. Throttle back to 1,000rpm, then perform the same checks on the second engine.

Before taxiing, confirm that brake pressure is not less than 120psi, and that the pressure head heater is on. Wave away the chocks. Taxi slowly, avoiding short radius turns. The aircraft must never be turned with one wheel locked.

Take-off checks
Check trim tabs (all neutral), mixture controls (normal, if manual), propeller controls (levers fully forward), fuel pressure balance cock (off), superchargers (medium), carburettor air intakes (cold), flaps (20° down), gills one-third open, oil cooler shutters (open as necessary, Mk III only), and throttle controls friction damper (as required). Set compass and synchronise directional gyro. Set altimeter to height of airfield above sea level. Clear the engines by opening up to 0lb boost against the brakes. Throttle back, release brakes, turn into wind and taxi forward a few yards to straighten the tail wheel. Open the throttles slowly, keeping straight using the rudder and differential use of the throttles. Raise the tail wheel early in the take-off run and ease the aircraft off the runway at not less than 85mph IAS. When safely airborne, apply the brakes to stop the wheels spinning and retract undercarriage. Increase speed to at least 115mph before climbing (the safety speed with 20° flap). At 400–500ft, raise the flaps. Reduce boost and rpm to climbing power, and climb away at 135mph IAS.

Landing checks
Check brake pressure (above 120psi), carburettor air intakes (cold), gills (closed), elevator trimming tabs (neutral), superchargers (medium), reduce speed to 140mph. Confirm undercarriage down and locked. Set mixture controls (normal, if manual), propeller controls (2,400rpm), nacelle tanks (on) and flaps (20° at 140mph to check even operation). Reduce speed to 120mph, then lower flaps fully on

the final approach, which should be made at 85–90mph, depending on weight of aircraft. Flare slightly – touch down on main wheels only.

After landing

Before taxiing, raise flaps and open gills. Allow engines to cool to below 230° while running at 1,200rpm, opening up gradually and evenly to not more than 1,500rpm, exercise the two-speed supercharger then return to medium. Open up gradually to -2lb boost then, over about five seconds, close the throttle smoothly and evenly until speed is down to 800-900rpm. Run at this speed for two minutes to operate the Worth oil dilution system. If an engine backfires during any part of the cooling procedure, it should be repeated (except for the exercising of the supercharger).

Next, for each engine in turn, pull out the slow-running cut-out and hold it until the engine has stopped, then switch off the ignition. After the second engine has stopped, switch off all electrical services, turn off the engine master cocks and close the gills. Prior to leaving the aircraft, ensure that the wheels are chocked appropriately for the prevailing wind conditions.

The gunner's view

It was the job of the gunners to protect the aircraft from enemy fighters, constantly scanning the sky in all directions to give maximum warning of attack. The rear turret, although usually colder, was generally preferred as it was easier to escape from (exit from the nose turret required another crew member to open the internal bulkhead) and the later four-gun rear turrets were (slightly) larger. On night operations, the front turret was often left unmanned, as

head-on attacks were uncommon. Gunners' parachutes were originally carried inside the fuselage, but later were placed within the turret. In case an emergency occurred, gunners were advised to vacate their turrets during take-off and landing, unless there was a direct threat to the airfield.

All Wellington turrets were fitted with .303 belt-fed Browning machine guns – these were found to be almost trouble free in service, problems only arising if rounds were not properly aligned in the ammunition belts. However, even with four guns, they offered a low weight of fire compared to the cannon of German fighters. A test burst was always fired en route to the target in case a jam had occurred.

The armourer was responsible for the guns and turrets being in good order, and loaded with the correct ammunition for the forthcoming operation. Typically, a gunner would visit the armoury and then check his turret several hours prior to the operation.

Gun turret drill (FN.5 turret, other turrets similar)
Pre-flight checks

On entering the turret, check that both ammunition tanks are present and loaded with the correct type. The arming cable is then fed over the gun and into the ammunition duct and down to the tank. The hook on the cable is attached to the end of the ammunition belt, with the hook pointing the same way as the bullets; pull the rounds up the duct, through the feed opening (the armourer may have already pulled the ammunition up and left it ready to load). Place the first round over the retaining pawl, close the breech cover, return the arming cable to its stowage pouch, and replace the

RIGHT The canvas bulkhead forward of the rear turret, with the emergency axe in its holder (right). *(Author)*

FAR RIGHT The side of the nose turret. The wide gap allowed the turret to rotate more than 100° to each side. *(Author)*

FAR LEFT The bulkhead door behind the nose turret. This had to be opened and closed by another crewmember, as the gunner could not do it himself. *(Author)*

LEFT Looking forwards from the rear turret. Note the control push rods on the port side. *(Author)*

ammunition tank covers. Finally, check that the fire/safe unit is set to 'safe'. Meanwhile, the ground crew thoroughly clean the turret Perspex – dirt could be mistaken for another aircraft.

Operational use

Enter the turret by opening the bulkhead and turret doors, reaching in to fold the safety harness upwards and backwards on to the ammunition tanks (to avoid sitting on them when climbing into the turret), then use the roof handrail to swing feet-first into the turret (rear gunners need to be careful not to touch the elevator bar).

Once in the turret, plug in the intercom (having put the plug into a pocket before getting into the turret) making sure that the plug is fully home, and call the pilot to check correct operation. Then reach back and close the fuselage bulkhead door then the turret doors (with pull-straps provided), left then right (in the case of the front turret, another member of the crew must close the bulkhead door) bolting them and checking that they are locked by leaning back on to the doors.

Do up the safety harness, and check that the reflector sight brightness is set appropriately.

Check both ammunition tanks by unclipping and removing the covers, and inspecting the base of the rounds to ensure that the ammunition is being fed properly; lids are then replaced and clipped shut. Check the arming cable and loading toggle, and return them to their stowage pouch, and check that the turret hand rotation is disengaged. If required, adjust the seat height by winding handles on both sides, returning the handles to their stowed positions. Unlock the turret by pulling up the locking plunger, and check for rotation,

elevation, and depression; and check operation of the firing gear.

Cock guns by hooking the cocking toggle (a short cable with a ring on one end and a T handle on the other) over the cocking stud and pulling it back; operate the trigger to release the rear sear, cock the guns again, and return the toggle to its stowage pouch. Set fire/safe unit to 'fire', fire test burst and report 'Guns OK' to the pilot.

End-of-flight drill

Centralise the turret and press home the rotation plunger, set the fire/safe unit to 'safe', switch off the reflector sight, then unload each gun by lifting the breech cover and pulling back the cocking stud with the loading toggle. Raise the transporter and remove the round from the face of the breechblock. Depress the rear sear release, thereby allowing the breechblock to fly forward. While the breech cover is raised, release the end of the ammunition belt from the retaining pawl. Press down the transporter and close the breech cover.

Prevent ammunition belts from slipping back into the tanks by folding them back over the top of the ducts. Unplug the intercom (remember to hold the dangling socket to prevent damage), put the jack into a pocket to avoid the wire trailing, then undo the safety harness, open the turret doors and exit the turret using the roof handrail. Close and lock the turret and bulkhead doors, collecting parachute before leaving the aircraft.

RIGHT **Looking rearwards from the mid-fuselage. An electrics board (left) and rest bunk (right) are ahead of the trailing edge frame, while beyond it can be seen the flare chute (left), Elsan toilet (right), and walkway to the rear turret.** *(Author)*

RIGHT **The first-aid kits, Elsan toilet, and rest bunk on the port side.** *(Author)*

ABOVE **Looking into the starboard bomb compartment through the rear window, with the bomb beam (left) and valance (right). The perforated plate (top) would have carried one of the flotation bags.** *(Author)*

Emergency drill

In case of crew injuries, first-aid kits and a rest bunk are available in the central fuselage area near the Elsan chemical toilet (the toilet was rarely used, because of problems with heavy flying suits, and pilots liked to 'take evasive action' if they heard a crewmember was on the toilet).

If the pilot decides the aircraft should be abandoned or ditched, he should open the bomb doors, jettison any small bomb containers, then jettison any remaining bombs, torpedoes, mines or other stores, then close the bomb doors. If time allows, fuel should also be jettisoned to reduce weight and fire risk, by unscrewing the air vent valve wheel on the left

of the instrument panel and then rotating the jettison valve wheel immediately above (later aircraft have only one valve control); 100 gallons can be discharged in 15–25sec, depending on flap position. The valves can be closed to stop the jettison and, if ditching, should be closed to preserve buoyancy.

The aircraft can be exited in flight via the entrance hatch in the bomb aimer's compartment (a foot lever on the starboard side opens it

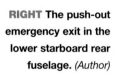

RIGHT **The push-out emergency exit in the lower starboard rear fuselage.** *(Author)*

FAR RIGHT **The emergency exit from the inside with its protective cover.** *(Author)*

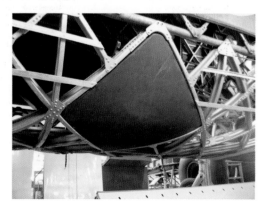

FAR LEFT 'R for Robert's' bombsight (inside) with downward identification light and Venturi (outside). *(Author)*

LEFT The cockpit canopy. The handle releases a catch to allow the two upper panels to hinge outwards. *(Author)*

independently of the release handle) or via the starboard side push-out panel (after removing the cover/guard). The rear gunner can exit his turret by turning it to the beam position then jettisoning the turret doors and rolling out backwards; if his parachute is stored in the fuselage ahead of the turret, he should exit the turret normally, retrieve his parachute, then use the starboard side exit. Front gunners cannot exit their turret to the side because of the proximity of the airscrews.

In the event of a crash-landing, the two windows in the top of the cockpit, hinged at the outboard side and held closed by a central lever, can be opened upwards. The astrodome on top of the fuselage can also be opened inwards for escape.

Ditching drill

The key to a successful ditching is crew training and discipline, as many functions need to be performed in a short space of time (typically less than three minutes), probably in the dark and with a damaged aircraft.

After committing to a ditching and jettisoning bombs and fuel, ensure that the bomb doors are closed again, both to smooth the contact with the water and to protect the flotation bags (see Chapter 3); if these are carried, they should be inflated five minutes before ditching (if possible, but not above 3,000ft) and inflation confirmed visually through the bomb bay rear windows. The bags in turn give support internally to the bomb doors during the ditching. If fitted, the ventral turret should be fully retracted, and the astro-hatch should be removed inwards in preparation for escape.

The pilot and rear gunner should remain at their stations, other crew moving into a seated position with their backs to the rear step in the cabin, in preparation for sudden deceleration (most ditching injuries happen to crew not in their ditching positions). It is important to approach the water at the slowest possible speed and as near to horizontal as possible, with 30° of flap lowered. Landing lights can be used at night to help judge height.

After ditching, the crew should exit the aircraft as quickly as possible via the nearest exit to the dinghy in the starboard engine nacelle, which should have inflated automatically.

BELOW Emergency equipment and exits. *(Crown Copyright)*

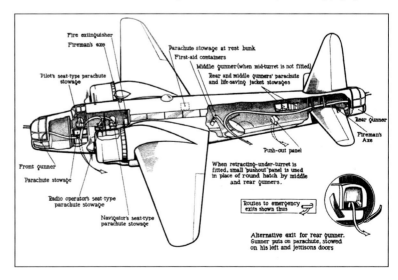

Chapter Seven

The Engineers' View

The apparent complexity of geodetic construction hid a structure that was both extremely resistant to damage and easy to repair, even with limited access to parts and workshop facilities. The Wellington's open structure and spacious airframe gave relatively easy access for maintenance and repair.

OPPOSITE Maintenance staff overhaul damaged Vickers Wellington Mk IC, T2470 'BU-K', of No 214 Squadron, inside a C-type hangar at Stradishall, Suffolk. *(IWM CH1416)*

RIGHT In June 1943 Leconfield in Yorkshire was home to 196 and 466 Squadrons, both equipped with the Wellington Mk X, one of which receives some attention to its Hercules engines in this view. Foaming tankards replace the more usual bomb symbols to indicate 14 successfully completed operations. *(IWM CH10247)*

Servicing and maintenance

BELOW Engine fitters overhaul one of the Bristol Pegasus XVIII radial engines of a 37 Squadron Wellington at Feltwell, 8 July 1940. An SBC with Wellington adapter is seen on the ground. *(IWM CH513)*

Maintenance of the Wellington was similar to other aircraft of the period and, once the war started, procedures evolved rapidly to deal with operational requirements. Often an aircraft would return in the early hours, and had to be repaired, rearmed, and made ready for another operation by late afternoon. An air test of each aircraft was conducted by the flight crew and any faults found had to be fixed to allow

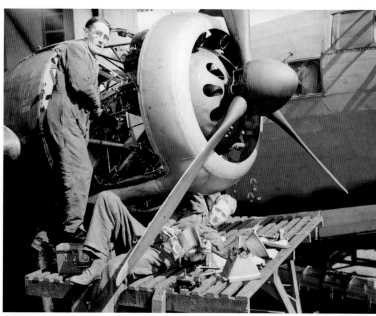

the pilot to sign off the Form 700 before the next operation. The groundcrews worked hard to keep the aircraft operational, often in harsh conditions – especially early in the war when there were fewer airfields with paved runways, and a shortage of hangarage meant that work was often carried out in the open. It was common to throw tarpaulins over the engines to act as a tent when working on them. Because of the fragile nature of the covering, groundcrew were required to wear plimsolls at all times when working on the aircraft – whatever the weather.

Daily inspections were carried out on operational aircraft, and further inspections were conducted at 25, 50 and 100 hours and other set intervals. The daily electrical inspection was as follows:

- Check battery (physical condition).
- Check lights (internal and external).
- Engine run-up to test generator and perform voltage and controls check.
- Check pitot head, gunsights, and electrical heaters.
- Replace any blown bulbs.

Electrical insulation was prone to damage by petrol, so extra care had to be taken to check wiring in and around the engines and fuel tanks.

Airframe life was not usually long enough to give any fatigue or corrosion problems, although

corrosion from sea air was reported in some coastal OTU aircraft. Some problems attributed to fatigue cracks were encountered in the main spar, leading to several instances of outer wings detaching in flight, requiring all Wellingtons to be checked. This involved removal of the outer wings, and if a problem was found the wing was replaced, otherwise the spar was fitted with a strengthening sleeve.

BELOW The rear of the pilot's instrument panel. *(Author)*

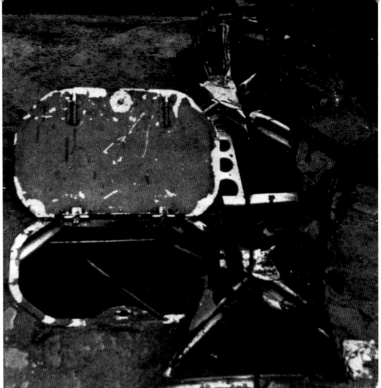

ABOVE LEFT Refitting a cylinder to the Pegasus on Fairey Swordfish LS326. *(Fly Navy Heritage Trust)*

ABOVE Barrage balloon damage to the wing of Mk IC R1459. The path of the cable as it sawed through the leading edge (top) and geodetics can be seen. It had cut through the forward pair of main spar tubes (and the fuel and hydraulics lines) before the cable snapped, and Ken Wallis and his crew were lucky to walk away from the crash-landing that followed. *(Ken Wallis)*

BELOW 'R for Robert' from behind. The horizontal stabiliser is the original (narrow) shape, and is partly hiding a large model of a DWI Wellington. *(Author)*

Re-arming drill

After landing, an aircraft must be ready to take to the air as quickly as possible in case of emergency, and tests to be run on the aircraft will require it to be fuelled and topped-up with oil; hence the refuelling squad arrive at the aircraft first.

Any remaining bombs are removed by the armourers. Engine fitters perform an engine check, making any necessary adjustments and repairs. Riggers examine the airframe and control surfaces, checking for combat damage, topping up hydraulic reservoirs and lubricating where necessary. Photographic equipment used to take photos of the target is reloaded and replaced, together with photographic flares. Crew oxygen is replenished by carefully replacing the bottles.

Guns are cleaned daily, the recoiling sections being removed from the turrets for this purpose. If they have not been fired, they can be simply cleaned by pulling through a piece of lightly-oiled flannelette. Once reassembled, the guns

and gunsight are harmonised by training the guns and sight on to a reduced-scale sighting board, checking the alignment of the individual guns on their respective spots on the board by looking through the barrels and the gunsight. Ammunition belts are passed through a belt-positioning machine to align each cartridge and are then fed into empty ammunition boxes for easy transport to the aircraft.

The following servicing times are quoted for Mk I aircraft:

- Refuel aircraft with standard equipment – 47 minutes.
- Rearm with ammunition – 25 minutes (four men).
- Change oxygen cylinders – 25 minutes.
- Remove and replace guns – 60 minutes (four men).
- Swing compass – 45–60 minutes.
- Change batteries – 15 minutes (not required if generators are working properly).

Once the aircraft has been checked appropriately, the aircrew take it up for a 20-minute test flight, during which engines, radio, guns, controls, bomb-release gear, and other parts are subjected to a working test. If no faults are found, it is ready for bombing-up on its return.

Bombing-up

Bombing-up is done in three main stages, the first two (collection of the bombs and fusing) by the station armourers, and the third (loading on to the aircraft) by squadron personnel.

Smaller bombs are manoeuvred beneath the bomb release that they are to be attached to, which is pulled down on its cable and fixed to the bomb suspension lug. Winch cables at the front positions are not long enough to load 250lb bombs from the ground, and these should be hoisted from the transport trolley or blocks. If the centre cell is used, it must be loaded and crutched first while easy access can be obtained from the outer cells.

A long crank handle is inserted through a hole in the fuselage side to engage with the winch (which is integral to the bomb beam) and the bomb is then manually winched up until the release slip is back in its housing. Note that the

BELOW Bombing-up.
(Jonathan Falconer collection)

winch has no ratchet so it must be held with both hands until the slip is locked in position. To prevent damage to the aircraft during winching, the bombs should be guided by the armourers who should take care not to stand beneath the bomb. The crutches are then adjusted and the fuse-setting control links connected between the safety collars of the nose and tail pistols and the fuse-setting control box. Small bomb containers (with Wellington adapter frame) are loaded in the same way as small bombs. The cocking operation of the electromagnetic unit is automatic, so testing is not usually necessary. However, it can be cocked by hand before hoisting the bomb, and the test lever then pressed.

For 1,000lb and 2,000lb bombs, the bomb carrier is placed on top of the bomb on the trolley, and a sling put around the bomb and secured to the release slip. The trolley is then manoeuvred beneath the winch cable in the aircraft, which is pulled down and attached to the carrier. The whole unit is then manually winched up into the bomb bay (usually done by a rigger and fitter under the supervision of an armourer), and the carrier located to the special bomb beam. The nose and tail crutches are adjusted to stop the bomb moving during flight, and then the fusing wire is fixed in position.

Finally, the armourer removes the safety pins from the pistols and stows them in the correct stowage in the aircraft; he then reports this to the bomb aimer and the armaments NCO.

Recovery of crashed aircraft

Many aircraft were damaged in forced landings and, where possible, repaired and returned to service. Vickers-Armstrongs working parties used custom-designed vehicles carrying a complete mobile workshop, including a converted bus concealing a set of sheer legs able to lift damaged aircraft. The aircraft was repaired in situ if possible and made ready for flight, sometimes requiring fields to be levelled and hedges removed to allow a take-off to be made. If more extensive work was required, the aircraft would be dismantled and taken to Weybridge, typically on a 'Queen Mary' articulated low-loader.

If an aircraft had made a wheels-up landing, it was lifted either using cantilever jacks under the inner wings or using airbags under the outer wing roots. When inflated from a compressor or air cylinder, these raised up the aircraft, allowing heavy bogies to be moved under the nacelles.

The aircraft could then be towed cautiously with ropes tied around the propeller hubs.

Damage to main gear was common, because of ground contact after the undercarriage had started retracting. This typically broke the retraction jack anchorage structure. Tail wheel damage was also frequent because of the 'tail down' attitude of the Wellington on landing which, with a bit of additional landing flare, resulted in a heavy contact. This typically required replacement of the lower section of the 85 and 90 frames.

Repairing damage

The geodetics occupied little space, so flak would often pass through the fuselage without hitting any structure. If structure was hit, every part was (in principle) repairable, although some repairs were best described as 'intelligent bodges'.

AP1578 B & C, Volume II, includes guidelines for formal classification of damage, and suggestions for repair, to most parts of the aircraft, which could be:

■ Minor – needing no attention.
■ Requiring repair by:
  • patching (i.e. covering damage with a strengthening section) or;
  • insertion (i.e. replacement of part of the geodetics). Damaged structure was cut out, usually midway between two node (crossing) points, and a new section (cut from an assembled panel and trimmed to give a 0.005in gap), was inserted and joined by a plate riveted around the geodetic profile. Small sections could also be replaced with wooden geodetics bolted to sound structure, and metal plates could be riveted on to strengthen weakened sections of structure.

■ Major – requiring replacement of the whole part.

The covering is prone to weathering damage, especially when used in tropical conditions, and is also easily damaged by air and ground crew. Damage to the covering can be easily repaired by cutting away any ragged edges and gluing patches over the holes, then doping over the patch. Ideally this is then painted to complete the camouflage, but unpainted patches are seen in many photographs of operational aircraft.

Badly damaged aircraft went to the Weybridge 'refurbishment line', which carried out more extensive repairs. Originally in a hangar beside the main factory, this was destroyed in the September 1940 bombing, and it moved to a Bellman hangar erected alongside the railway. It took approximately six weeks to restore an aircraft to flying condition following a wheels-up landing. In this way, around 2,000 damaged aircraft were returned to service.

Aircraft damaged beyond repair were salvaged for parts, although aircraft which had been burnt were scrapped and the metal reclaimed.

Conclusion

Beaten to the glory by fighters like the Spitfire and Hurricane, and outshone by later bombers like the sleek Mosquito and heavier Lancaster, the Wellington's contribution to Allied victory is sometimes overlooked. However, its unique construction was ideal for mass production and easy repair, and earned the aircraft an unequalled reputation for ruggedness. Its versatility saw it used in more roles, and in more theatres of war, than any other British heavy aircraft.

N2980 and MF628 remain as the sole exemplars of geodetic construction, standing as fitting tributes to an aircraft that was the best of its contemporaries. The Bomber Command Memorial in London's Green Park uses geodetics in its roof to commemorate the role of the Wellington, which remains the most numerous multi-engined British aircraft ever built, and its place in history is secure.

ABOVE Form follows function in the geodetics of the rear fuselage of 'R for Robert'. (Author)

BELOW An example of an 'insertion' repair in the geodetic structure. (Crown Copyright via The National Archives)

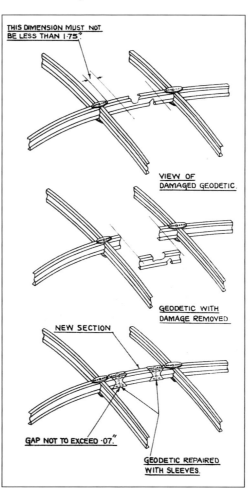

Appendix 1

Glossary and abbreviations

A&AEE Aircraft & Armaments Experimental Establishment (originally at Martlesham Heath, later at Boscombe Down).

ADS Atmospheric Diving Suit – a hardened, articulated diving suit, allowing a diver to work at depth for extended periods at normal atmospheric pressure, thus avoiding the need for decompression.

AI Airborne Interception radar, typically used by night-fighters to home on to targets.

ASI Air Speed Indicator.

ASV Air-to-Surface Vessel radar, typically used to home on to shipping targets.

Boost The amount of additional pressure created by a supercharger.

CCDU Coastal Command Development Unit (based initially at Carew Cheriton and later at Ballykelly, Tain, Dale and Angle).

Cookie Codename for the 4,000lb HC cylindrical blast bomb.

DR Direct Reading – a gyro-based compass which gave a more accurate reading than the standard magnetic compass.

DTD Directorate of Technical Development (part of the Air Ministry).

DWI Directional Wireless Installation – codename for aerial minesweeping gear fitted to a Wellington for exploding magnetic sea mines.

ELINT Electronic Intelligence – listening for (and occasionally jamming) radio and radar signals.

Feathering Turning propeller blades edge-on to the airflow to minimise drag, usually following an engine failure.

FN Frazer-Nash – designers of power-operated gun turrets.

Gardening Codename for minelaying operations.

Gee A navigational aid, commonly fitted to bombers, by which an aircraft could locate its position.

GP General Purpose – the standard bomb type with a cast casing.

HC High Capacity (i.e. high charge-to-weight ratio) – a type of blast bomb with a thin sheet metal casing.

hp Horsepower – a measure of engine power.

HT High Tension (i.e. high voltage).

IAS Indicated Air Speed (i.e. speed as measured by the aircraft instruments, which varies – according to conditions – from True Air Speed).

Lindholme gear A collection of survival equipment packaged for air-dropping to ditched aircrew.

LT Low Tension (i.e. low voltage).

MTB Motor Torpedo Boat.

MU Maintenance Unit.

Nickel Codename for operations to drop propaganda leaflets.

Oboe A navigational aid, commonly used by Pathfinder aircraft, by which an aircraft could locate a target position.

OTU Operational Training Unit.

psi Pounds per square inch – a measurement of pressure.

RAE Royal Aircraft Establishment (at Farnborough and other locations).

Recuperator Fluid reservoir which evens out changes in pressure in the hydraulic system.

ROV Remotely Operated Vehicle – a miniature submarine with cameras, controlled from the surface.

RP Rocket Projectile.

R/T Radio Telegraphy – sending voice messages by radio.

SAP Semi-Armour Piercing – a bomb type with a thicker casing than GP bombs.

SIS Secret Intelligence Service (MI6) – engaged on dropping and supplying agents in enemy-occupied Europe.

Supercharger A device to increase the inlet pressure of a piston engine to boost its power.

SWG Standard Wire Gauge – a scale used for measuring the thickness of wire and sheet metal.

TBO Time Between Overhauls – a measure of the service life of an engine.

Turbocharger An exhaust-driven supercharger.

VAX1 Vickers-Armstrongs Extension One – the Weybridge secondary production site at Smith's Lawn in Windsor Great Park.

W/T Wireless Telegraphy – sending Morse code messages by radio.

Appendix 2

Manufacture and conversions

WELLINGTON PRODUCTION MARKS AND PROTOTYPES

Mark	Vickers Type	Description	Engines	Weybridge	Broughton	Blackpool	Total	1st Flight	Production Delivery
Prototype	271	B.9/32 prototype K4049	Pegasus X	1	0	0	1	15 Jun 1936	
I	285	Pre-production L4212, L4213	Pegasus XX then XVIII	2	0	0	2	23 Dec 1937	
I	290/403	Production	Pegasus XVIII	176	3	0	179		Oct 1938–Aug 1939
IA	408/412	Production	Pegasus XVIII	170	17	0	187		Nov 1939–Apr 1940
IC	415	Production	Pegasus XVIII	1,052	1,583	50	2,685		Mar 1940–Oct 1942
II	298	Prototype L4250	Merlin X	1	0	0	1	3 Mar 1939	
B.II	406	Production	Merlin X	401	0	0	401		Oct 1940–Jun 1942
III	299	Prototype L4251	Hercules III	2	0	0	2	19 May 1939	
B.III	417	Production	Hercules III or XI	0	737	780	1,517		Nov 1940–Oct 1942
IV	410	Prototype R1220	Twin Wasp R-1830	0	1	0	1	Dec 1940	
B.IV	424	Production	Twin Wasp R-1830	0	219	0	219		Dec 1940–May 1942
V	421/436	1st prototype R3298	Hercules III then XI	1	0	0	1	Sep 1940/Mar 1942	
V	407	2nd prototype R3299	Hercules VIII	1	0	0	1	Nov 1940	
V	426	3rd prototype W5796	Hercules VIII	1	0	0	1		
VI	431	Prototype W5795	Merlin 60	1	0	0	1	Nov 1941	
B.VI	442	Production	Merlin 60	28	0	0	28		Oct 194–May 1942
B.VIG	449	Production	Merlin 60	35	0	0	35		May 1942–Mar 1943
GR.VIII	429	Production	Pegasus XVIII	394	0	0	394		Oct 1940–Oct 1942
B.X	440	Production	Hercules VI or XVI	0	2,434	1,369	3,803	Jul 1942	Aug 1942–Oct 1945
XI	454	ASV II prototype MP502	Hercules VI	1	0	0	1		
XI	459	ASV III prototype MP545	Hercules XVI	1	0	0	1		
GR.XI	458	Production	Hercules VI or XVI	103	0	75	178		Feb 1943–Nov 1943
GR.XII	455	Production	Hercules VI or XVI	50	8	0	58		Dec 1942–Aug 1943
GR.XIII	466	Production	Hercules XVII	42	0	803	845		Jun 1943–Jun 1944
GR.XIV	467	Production	Hercules XVII	53	538	249	840		May 1943–Jul 1945
T.XVIII	490	Production	Hercules XVII	0	0	80	80		Oct 1944–Oct 1945
Total built				2,516	5,540	3,406	11,462		

CONVERTED MARKS

Mark	Vickers Type	Description	Engines	Notes
IX	437	Transport	Various	Unknown number of conversions from several early marks
C.XV		Troop transport	Pegasus XVIII	18 conversions from Mk IA
C.XVI		Troop transport	Various	54 conversions from Mk IC, 1 conversion from Mk III
T.XVII	487	AI radar trainer	Hercules VI or XVI	9 conversions from Mk XI
T.XIX		Trainer	Hercules VI or XVI	6 conversions from B.X (18 more cancelled)
T.10	619	Trainer	Hercules VI or XVI	270 conversions from B.X (post-war, hence Arabic numeral)

OTHER NOTABLE CONVERSIONS AND PROTOTYPES

Mark	Vickers Type	Description	Engines	Notes
IB	409	Mk IB proposed as Mk IA with improved armament	Pegasus XVIII	Cancelled
II	416	Dorsal S gun experimental, later with twin fins	Hercules VI or XVI	1 prototype conversion from Mk II L4250
IA	418	DWI Mk I – Ford V8	Pegasus XVIII	4 conversions from Mk IA
Various	419	DWI Mk II – DH Gipsy VI	Pegasus XVIII	4 conversions from Type 418, 11 conversions from Mk I, 1 conversion from Mk IC
Various	423	4,000lb HC bomb conversion		Numerous conversions from several marks; prototypes were W5389, W5399, W5400
IC	428	DWI Mk III – Leigh Light experimental	Hercules XI	1 prototype conversion from Type 419 P9223
VII	430	Mk VII proposed as Mk II with improved engines	Merlin XX	1 prototype conversion from Mk II T2545, cancelled before completion
VIII	435	Turbinlite experimental	Pegasus XVIII	1 prototype conversion from Mk VIII T2977
II	439	Nose S gun experimental	Merlin X	1 prototype conversion from Mk II Z8416
I	445	Test bed – Whittle W2B/23 jet in tail	Merlin X then XX	1 conversion from Mk II Z8570
IA	451	Auxiliary Generator Plant (AGP) test bed	Pegasus XVIII	1 conversion from Mk IA N2963
III	452	Golf mine (bouncing bomb) experimental	Hercules III	1 conversion from Mk III BJ895
II	470	Test bed – Whittle W2B jet in tail	Merlin 62	1 conversion from Mk II W5389 with wings from Mk VI DR524
II	486	Test bed – Whittle W2/700 jet in tail	Merlin 62	1 conversion from Mk II W5518 with wings from Mk VI W5802
X	478	Test bed – Hercules 100	Hercules 100	1 conversion from B.X LN718
X	602	Test bed – Dart turboprop	Dart	1 conversion from B.X LN715
Various		Glider tug experimental		At least four aircraft – X3286 (Mk III), X9790 and DV942 (Mk IC), HE731 (B.X)

Vickers Types 295, 296, 297, 403, 412, 434, 443, 448, 450, 475, 477, 481, 603, 608, and 638 were also assigned to Wellington variants, most of which were not produced.

Different sources give different numbers for each mark built/converted; the data above are derived from a combination of sources with the details of each individual aircraft cross-checked to resolve inconsistencies. Andrews and Morgan's *Vickers Aircraft since 1908* gives the total number of Wellingtons as 11,461 but their own data totals to 11,462. It is estimated that production of spare parts was equivalent to an additional 1,000 complete aircraft. Orders placed for a further 2,700 Wellingtons of various marks were cancelled.

Orders placed for a further 600 Warwicks of various marks were cancelled. All Warwicks were built at Weybridge.

WARWICK PRODUCTION MARKS AND PROTOTYPES

Mark	Vickers Type	Description	Engines	Weybridge	1st Flight
Prototype	284	K8178	Vulture II	1	13 Aug 1939
Prototype	401/427	L9704	Centaurus/Double Wasp	1	5 Apr 1940/Jul 1941
Prototype	413	BV216	Centaurus IV	1	Jun 1943
B.I	444	Bomber, used as test beds	Double Wasp	16	
C.I (BOAC)	456	Transport	Double Wasp	14	
ASR.I	462	ASR Lindholme	Double Wasp	40	
ASR.A	462	ASR lifeboat + Lindholme	Double Wasp	10	
ASR.B	462	ASR lifeboat + Lindholme + ASV Mk II	Double Wasp	20	
ASR.C/ASR.I	462	ASR multi-configuration	Double Wasp	205	
ASR.VI	485	ASR multi-configuration	Double Wasp	95	
GR.II	469	ASV Mk III + Leigh Light	Centaurus VII	118	
GR.II Met	611	Meteorological equipped	Centaurus VII	14	
GR.V	474	ASV Mk III + Leigh Light	Centaurus VII	211	Apr 1944
C.III	460	Transport	Double Wasp	100	
Total built				**846**	

Vickers Types 400, 411, 422, 433, 438, 468, 472, 473, 474, 484, 497, 600, 605, and 606 were also assigned to Warwick variants, many of which were not produced.

Appendix 3

Squadrons operating geodetic aircraft

The 'notch' in the top graph between July 1939 and July 1940 is remarkable, and is probably because of later marks of Wellington re-equipping squadrons already flying the type (rather than going to new squadrons), and the formation of OTUs, which typically had three times as many aircraft as front line squadrons.

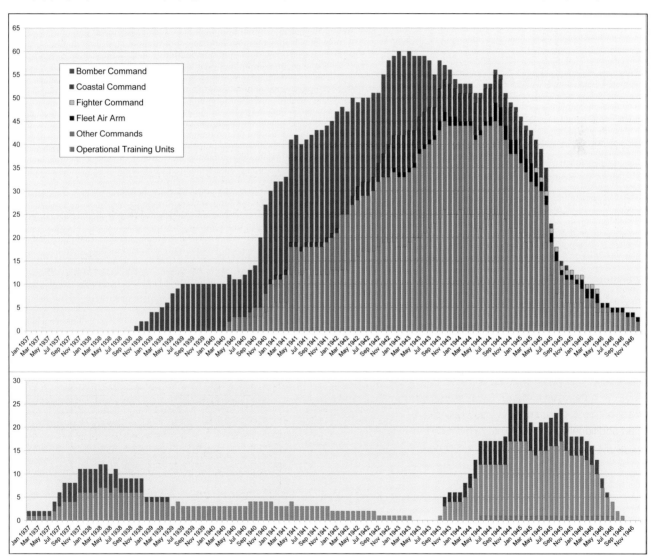

Appendix 4

Bibliography

Andrews, C.F. and Morgan, E.B., *Vickers Aircraft since 1908* (Putnam, 1988)

Barfield, Norman, *Vickers Aircraft* (Chalford, 1997)

——, *Broughton: From Wellington to Airbus* (Tempus, 2001)

Bowman, Martin, *Wellington: The Geodetic Giant* (Airlife, 1998)

Bowyer, Chaz, *The Wellington Bomber* (William Kimber, 1986)

——, *Wellington at War* (Ian Allan, 1982)

Franks, Norman, *Dark Sky, Deep Water* (Grub Street, 1999)

Halley, James, *The Squadrons of the Royal Air Force* (Air-Britain, 1980)

Holmes, Robin, *One of Our Aircraft: the Story of 'R for Robert' the Loch Ness Wellington* (Quiller Press, 1991)

Lumsden, Alec, *Wellington Special* (Ian Allan, 1974)

——, *British Piston Aero-Engines and their Aircraft* (Crowood, 2003)

Middlebrook, Martin and Everitt, Chris, *The Bomber Command War Diaries* (Midland Publishing, 1996)

Morpurgo, Jack E., *Barnes Wallis* (St Martin's, 1972; Penguin, 1973; Ian Allan, revised, 1981)

Murray, Iain R., *Bouncing-Bomb Man: The Science of Sir Barnes Wallis* (Haynes, 2009)

——, *Dam Busters Manual* (Haynes, 2011)

Robertson, Bruce, *British Military Aircraft Serials 1912–1966* (Ian Allan, 1968)

Webster, Charles and Frankland, Noble, *The Strategic Air Offensive Against Germany 1939–1945* (HMSO, 1961)

BELOW No photographs are known to exist of a 4,000lb HC 'Cookie' onboard a Wellington. Norman Parker built this model to demonstrate how the bomb protruded from the bomb bay. *(Norman Parker)*

Appendix 5

Useful contacts

Brooklands Museum
Home to Wellington N2980 'R for Robert' and many other exhibits from the birthplace of British aviation and motorsport
Brooklands Road,
Weybridge,
Surrey KT13 0QN
01932 857381
www.brooklandsmuseum.com

Rolls-Royce Heritage Trust
Custodians of the heritage of Rolls-Royce and Bristol engines
Main Office:
Rolls-Royce plc,
PO Box 31,
Derby DE24 8BJ
01332 248181
www.rolls-royce.com/about/heritage

Bristol Branch/Sir Roy Fedden Heritage Centre, PO Box 3, Filton, Bristol BS34 7QE (visitors by appointment only)
0117 979 1234
www.rolls-royce.com/about/heritage/
heritage_trust/branches/bristol_
branch.jsp

RAF Museum
Home to Wellington MF628 and many other military aircraft exhibits. MF628 is undergoing restoration at Cosford and is expected to return to Hendon in 2015.

Hendon site: Grahame Park Way,
London NW9 5LL
020 8205 2266
www.rafmuseum.org.uk/london

Cosford site: Shifnal, Shropshire TF11 8UP
01902 376200
www.rafmuseum.org.uk/cosford

Barnes Wallis Memorial Trust
Dedicated to preserving the memory of Sir Barnes Wallis and his work.
www.barneswallistrust.org

BELOW Many Wellingtons were lost on training flights. L7845 was an early Broughton-built Mk IC, from 20 OTU at Lossiemouth, which crashed on the Angus hills in 1942 following an engine failure. Only the tail gunner survived. *(Author)*

Index

Three DWI Wellingtons flying in 'V' formation at Boscombe Down.
(Crown Copyright via The National Archives)